Macmillan Drama Anthologies

Series editor: Cecily O'Neill

Sepia and Song

a collection of historical documentaries by
David Foxton

...pshire RG21 2XS

...atives
th...

Printe... ...g Kong

British Library Cataloguing in Publication Data
Foxton, David
Sepia and song: a collection of historical documentaries.
I. Title
822'.914 PR6056.09/
ISBN 0–333–40923–X

Contents

Preface

Macmillan Drama Anthologies

Macmillan Drama Anthologies offer a series of lively and stimulating play scripts to be read in class or presented for performance. The series is aimed at a range of age-groups, from middle school to upper secondary level, and will include scripts in a variety of genres – documentaries, musicals, and radio and TV adaptations. The plays are accompanied by source material and advice on presentation. Follow-up ideas for improvisation, written work and discussion are included so that work on the scripts can be extended in the English or drama lesson.

Sepia and Song

The plays in this volume are documentaries for musical production, directed towards the middle years of the secondary school. They were devised by the author directly from his work with youth theatre groups. Each play takes an historical incident as its starting-point, and uses a music-hall style and suggestions for accessible and familiar songs to create lively and often thought-provoking entertainment.

With their large casts, humour and broad characterisation, these short plays would be enjoyable to read in class. Since they do not rely for their success on elaborate costumes or sets or on a few 'star' performers, they are ideal for performance in drama clubs or to school audiences, as pieces for presentation in drama examinations, or to video or tape-record as a special project. They will be especially useful to the teacher seeking material for all-girl groups. The scripts are sufficiently flexible to allow scope for improvisation by the group, or for the inclusion of performers with special musical or dramatic skills.

Acknowledgements

The author and publishers wish to thank the following who have kindly given permission for the use of copyright material:

CBS Songs for 'That's my Weakness Now' © Lawrence Wright Music Co. Ltd, 'Ain't She Sweet' © Lawrence Wright Music Co. Ltd and 'Nobody's Sweetheart', © Lawrence Wright Music Co. Ltd.

EMI Music Publishing Ltd for 'Fall in and Follow Me' © 1910 B. Feldman & Co. Ltd, 'I Was a Good Little Girl 'till I Met You' © 1914 Francis Day & Hunter Ltd, 'Who were you with Last Night' © 1912 B. Feldman & Co. Ltd, 'Any Old Iron' © 1911 Herman Darewski Music Pub. Co., 'Put me Amongst the Girls' © 1907 B. Feldman & Co. Ltd, 'The Ship I Love' © 1893 Herman Darewski Music Pub. Co. and 'Pack Up Your Troubles (in Your Old Kit Bag)' © 1915 Francis Day and Hunter Ltd.

The author and publishers wish to acknowledge the following photograph sources:
David Foxton, page 118; C. B. Jackson, pages 40 and 78; Popperfoto, pages 33, 71, 113; John Topham Picture Library, pages 1 and 8.

Every effort has been made to trace all the copyright holders but if any have been inadvertently overlooked the publishers will be pleased to make the necessary arrangement at the first opportunity.

A Memory of Lizzie

Lizzie Borden

Introduction

It is often said that children can be very cruel: perhaps it takes time to learn to be kind. Certainly it is interesting how many children's stories and nursery rhymes have cruel, even vicious, elements. It is not hard to make a list of examples – Hansel and Gretel being fattened up by the witch because she intends to eat them, and then the two of them pushing the witch into her own oven; Rumpelstiltskin tearing himself in half when his name was correctly guessed; the old man who wouldn't say his prayers who is taken by his left leg and thrown down the stairs in 'Goosey, goosey, gander' – you may be able to think of more examples.

It is also said that we all tend to find stories of murder to be fascinating. Perhaps the more horrific or unusual they are the more fascinating they become to us – certainly the newspapers seem to support such an opinion. So it is interesting to imagine the childhood of someone who in adult life became one of the most celebrated of murderers – Lizzie Borden. All the more interesting too since her crime has itself become the subject of a children's rhyme:

> Lizzie Borden took an axe
> And gave her mother forty whacks
> When she saw what she had done
> She gave her father forty-one.

Yet despite the insistence of the rhyme Lizzie was in fact acquitted of the murders. The jury found her not guilty of the murder of her mother and father in Fall River, Massachusetts, USA, on 4 August 1892. No other person was ever charged with the crimes, and indeed quite soon after the verdict the population of Fall River were asking themselves, if Lizzie did not do it, who did? – and they could not suggest an alternative culprit.

Those whose job it is to solve crimes always say, in books, in films, and in real life that there has to be a motive for murder. Lizzie Borden might have been considered as having a motive to kill her 'mother', for this was in fact her stepmother and there was no love lost between her and Lizzie and her elder sister, Emma. Emma called her new mother 'Abby' but Lizzie called her 'Mrs Borden', refused to eat at the same table with her, and spoke to her only when it was essential. Mister Borden was a wealthy man, but the family lived frugally and certainly Lizzie resented her stepmother being in line for the family fortune; she firmly believed that Mrs Borden was only after her father's riches. There was never any suggestion that she was a cruel stepmother, as in 'The Babes in the Wood', though she was strict; at the time her father remarried, Lizzie was five. Also at the time of the marriage Mrs Borden had a sister only one year old, and it may have complicated the relationships in the Borden home when Mrs Borden lavished affection on her infant sister rather than her new stepchildren. But even if Lizzie's jealousy might have driven her to attack her stepmother, there seems little reason why on the same day, within a few hours, she should also kill her father. Both were killed with an axe, and despite the ferocity of the killings no blood was found on Lizzie or any of her clothes; the axe, when discovered, had been thoroughly cleaned – but there had been no hurried washing done by Lizzie, though some clothing had been burnt in a downstairs store. Lizzie was certainly alone in the house at the time of the murders. Outwardly the family was thought of as quiet, settled and, though a little retiring, rather ordinary.

Lizzie continued to live in Fall River after the murders. She became something of a recluse, living alone and probably whispered about, until she died in 1927, aged 67. She never spoke or wrote about the events of 1892, she never volunteered any information that might have thrown light on the whole affair. Lizzie Borden is the most notorious murderer – who wasn't!

What might she have been like as a child? This play looks at a scene in the school-life of Lizzie Borden; amid the arguments, games and petty quarrels of a school playground are interspersed quotations from both Lizzie and others, twenty years later – from the murder enquiry. We use the term 'flashback' when a play or film shows scenes involving the characters in events happening earlier than the play or film itself. In this play we have 'flash-forwards' – not predictions but actual, factual commentaries.

At the end of the play the two areas of reality and 'flashforward' come together. Briefly we see Lizzie, the child, as Lizzie the murderer.

Staging the play

On stage, whether you choose to present this play on a conventional stage or in-the-round, the essential element that you need to create is that of a school playground at playtime.

Perhaps the best suggestion that could be given with regard to the acting of this play would be that you should observe some young children playing in the playground of a primary school. Although Lizzie and her fellow pupils are actually aged about 12, it would not be unreasonable to suggest that in the 1870s the average 12-year-old was less mature than a

12-year-old today. Consider what games they might play in addition to those suggested in the script, for there are times when the children are spread throughout the playground area, coming together for scenes that focus individual characters – rather in the way that a fight in a playground becomes an immediate focus of attention. The games need to be accurate to the period of the play and, from an audience point of view, you would do well to select games that are very visual and broad, e.g. 'tag', playing with a hoop, etc.

The director will need to select some system whereby the 'commentaries' or 'flashforwards' are 'pointed' – that is, given the necessary prominence. The script suggests the use of spotlights on individual characters while the rest of the cast 'freeze'. If no spotlights are available then perhaps the 'freeze' alone would work, but you must ensure complete stillness in these scenes for the slightest movement by one of the cast who should be 'frozen' will destroy the whole effect. You should always remember that someone in the audience will be watching each member of the cast. Audiences think that 'freezing' is easy – just because they have played 'statues' at some time. Well, it isn't and it will need careful rehearsal.

The play is about Americans, and therefore the ideal would be to try using an American accent. Apart from the 'commentary' sections most lines are short and should not give too many problems when adopting such an accent, but be prepared for laughs when inevitable mistakes happen. Keep an eye open for rhythms in the dialogue particularly during the skipping sequences.

The actual staging can be extremely simple. There is no absolute need for scenery as such. However, it is easier to group people on stage if there is at least one level slightly higher than the stage level. You might use a set of steps up to a 'school doorway' and a length of fencing as your set. Other settings might include a wall with 'graffiti' on it against which a ball can be bounced as part of a game.

Costumes can be kept simple. Girls will need a period apron or pinafore over a longish dress or blouse and skirt. Boys can wear jeans and a suitable shirt. Although originally played with an all-girl cast, the casting can be a combination of boys and girls – though the parts of Lizzie and Rachel must be female.

Your general lighting should suggest a sunny day over the whole stage. If it is possible to spotlight the 'flashforward' commentaries you might try a blue spot to give a rather 'ghostly' effect. These sections can all be played in the same spotlight if the director wishes it, or could be spread about the stage with different spotlights.

There are no sound effects required, but the cast must be prepared to sing. The use of 'Oranges and Lemons' as the introductory music could be criticised as being more an English children's song than an American one, but since Massachusetts has often been considered rather 'English' in its outlook, perhaps this is acceptable.

A Memory of Lizzie

The characters

Ann or Aaron
Barbara or Bernard
Christy or Colin
Dorothy or David
Eliza or Edward
Frances or Francis
Georgina or George
Hortense or Henry
Irma or Ian
Jo or Joe
Kathy or Keith
Lizzie Borden
May or Michael
Rachel Brayton

Apart from Lizzie and Rachel, the parts can be male or female and names altered accordingly, as above.

The Borden house in Fall River, Massachusetts

Auditorium lights fade down slowly: we hear children's voices singing – if it is a proscenium stage they are still behind the main curtain, if an open stage then the cast enter, singing, to their positions.

Children: Oranges and lemons
Say the bells of St Clements,
You owe me five farthings
Say the bells of St Martins.
When will you pay me?
Say the bells of Old Bailey.
When I grow rich
Say the bells of Shoreditch.
When will that be?
Say the bells of Stepney.
I'm sure I don't know
Says the great bell of Bow.
Here comes a candle
To light you to bed
And here comes a chopper
to chop off your head
Chop
Chop
Chop
CHOP

(*During the song the main curtain opens, or the lights come up if on an open stage, showing figures in silhouette playing the game of 'Oranges and Lemons' in a small American schoolyard – Massachusetts in about 1871/2.*

Lizzie Borden is caught on the fourth chop. She is normally very sure of herself but now she screams and a spotlight comes up on Lizzie held between two other children, Ann and Barbara; all are frozen except Lizzie.)

Lizzie: 'My full name is Lizzie Andrew Borden and I am 32 years of age. I have always lived in Fall River. My mother died when I was two. My father married my stepmother when I was five. The day they were killed I had on a blue dress. I went to school in Fall River . . . . . twenty years ago.'

(*Full lights up: spotlight goes out. Break the freeze.*)

Lizzie (*Breaking away*): Let me go . . . . Let me go . . . . Why've you caught me? Let me go . . .

Ann: It's only a game, Lizzie.

Barbara: An' you was caught fair and square.

Lizzie: No I wasn't, you made it be me. . . . You all wanted it to be me that was caught.

Barbara: Come on, Lizzie – y'know that's not so.

Lizzie: It is! It is! It's always me that ends up getting caught – never anyone else. I ain't gonna play any more.

(*She exits stage left. The others disperse around the 'playground' area and might pick up items for other games; e.g. a ball, a hoop, a whip and top.*)

Barbara: What's the matter with her now?

Christy: Leave her be – she'll come round.

Ann: Never plays fair . . . .

Dorothy: Can't take a joke – never could.

Eliza: Thinks too much of herself.

Dorothy: Just 'cos she's a Borden – thinks she owns the whole place.

Frances: Thinks she owns the whole world.

Dorothy: Lizzie Borden can't take a joke.

Eliza: She ain't got no sense of humour – that's a fact.

Ann: It's 'cos she's an only child, my ma says.

Christy: Well that ain't so – 'cos she's got a sister.

Georgina: Yeah she has – I seen her.

Barbara: Older sister she is!

Frances: Much older.

Barbara: Reckon she's almost as old as my ma.

Christy: Nope, she's about 10 years older than Lizzie.

Children (*Incredulously*): Well, that's really old.
As old as that!
(etc.)

Georgina: Must be all of twenty-some.

Dorothy: Wow – fancy bein' as old as that!

Ann: And Lizzie's got no ma.

Frances: Course she has.

Georgina: Yeah she has – I seen *her* too . . . .

Ann: No you haven't – she's her stepmother.

Hortense: What's that, then?

Georgina: Well, she looked like a real ma to me.

Ann: Well – it's when your real mother dies and your father marries again. His new wife then's your stepmother.

Barbara: I read about 'em.

Ann: When?

Christy: Where?

Barbara: In a book . . . a storybook.

Christy: What, about the Bordens?

Barbara: Nah! About stepmothers.

Ann: They're wicked and mean.

Irma: Who says so?

Barbara: This book said it – said they was never as kind as a real mother – they was cruel and wicked and . . .

(*Lizzie re-enters from the left and a spotlight picks her up; the rest of the cast freeze. The main stage lights dim.*)

Lizzie: 'I did not regard her as my mother, though she came to the house when I was young. I decline to say whether my relations between her and myself were those of mother and daughter or not. I called her Mrs Borden. She was not my mother. She was my stepmother. My mother was dead. I was a child.'

(*Full lights up: spotlight out. Break the freeze.*)

Lizzie: . . . and in 'The Babes in the Wood' she leaves them to die.

Georgina: Leaves who?

Lizzie: . . . leaves the little children – out in the forest to die 'cos she didn't love 'em – didn't want 'em – 'cos they weren't hers.

Eliza: That was 'Hansel and Gretel'.

Lizzie: Not this one. That's another story – only goes to show how *all* stepmothers is really awful.

(*The children group slowly round Lizzie, the focus of attention.*)

Barbara: Is yours, Lizzie?

Ann: Has she left you out to die yet?

Christy: Course she hasn't – y'can see she hasn't – Lizzie's here with us, isn't she?

Hortense: Tell us about Hansel and Gretel, then, Lizzie . . .

Irma: Yeah tell us.

Lizzie: Y'know the story.

Hortense: You tell it, Lizzie . . . you c'n tell it real scary.

Lizzie: Well, once upon a time there was this wicked stepmother who had two little stepchildren and she wanted to kill 'em, so that she wouldn't have to look after them no more. And so that their father would only have her to love.

(*Main stage lights dim, a spotlight picks up Georgina: the rest of the cast freeze.*)

Georgina: 'Two years after the death of his first wife and some 27 years before the killings, Andrew Jackson Borden married Abby Durfee Gray. The new Mrs Borden was 37 and had a sister who at the time of her marriage was only one year old. The relationship of the sisters was, because of the age difference, far more that of a mother and daughter than of sisters. Rebuffed in her home by her stepdaughters, childless herself, Abby Borden lavished her affection and attention on her sister.'

(*Main stage lights back up, spotlight out. Break the freeze.*)

Irma (*Moving closer to Lizzie*): Tell us about the witch too, Lizzie.

Hortense: Was she a stepmother?

Jo: An' how she was going to eat them.

Hortense: Like she was a caramel.

Ann: It's cannibal . . . and anyway she didn't eat 'em 'cos they got away.

Eliza: She lived in a house made of cookies and cake.

Frances: Yeah and the roof was all sugar.

Eliza: No – it was marzipan – I remember.

Frances: What's that?

Eliza: I don't know – but I remember that's what it was made of.

Frances: I tell you it was sugar – like icing.

Lizzie: Don't you wanna hear more about the wicked stepmother?

Frances: Sugar and spice.

Eliza: Marzipan.

Frances: Sugar and spice.

Dorothy (*Shouting them down, to end the argument*): And all things nice, that's what little girls are made of.

(*Pause*)

Lizzie: Don't you care how bad she was?

Christy: C'mon let's play ball.

(*They form a circle to play 'pig in the middle'. Lizzie does not join in but wanders away right.*)

Christy: C'mon, Lizzie, you play.
Dorothy: C'mon.
Eliza: Wanna play, Lizzie?
Georgina: You can if you want. (etc.)

(*Ad lib. from the others as well.*)

Lizzie: No – you ain't gonna catch me out again. You ain't gonna make a fool of me, any more. I'm not gonna be caught again.

(*Stage lights dim. A spotlight picks up Frances, the rest of the cast freeze.*)

Frances: 'Once Lizzie Borden was entertaining friends of hers. Mrs Borden's cat kept walking in the room and each time Lizzie put the cat out, sure enough, in he'd come again. Lizzie Borden finally excused herself and went downstairs taking the cat with her – she put the poor thing on the chopping-block and chopped its head off. Mrs Borden wondered for days where the cat was – all she talked about. Finally Lizzie said, "*You go downstairs and you'll find your cat*".'

(*Main stage lights back up, spotlight out. Break the freeze.*)

Lizzie (*Says or sings, moving to centre*):
I love little pussy
Her coat is so warm
And if I don't hurt her
She'll do me no harm,
So I'll not pull her tail
Nor drive her away
But pussy and I very gently will play.

(*The game has stopped during this song, the children have obviously been talking and whispering in small groups.*)

Irma: Go on . . . you ask her.

Jo: Why me?

Dorothy: Go on . . . dare you to.

Irma: Hey Lizzie, c'm here.

Lizzie: No, you c'm here.

Dorothy: Come on, Lizzie.

Lizzie: What d'you want?

Irma: Go ask her, Eliza.

Kathy: Yeah . . . go on. (*Pushing Eliza forward*)

(*Eliza approaches Lizzie and whispers to her.*)

Lizzie: No I shan't . . .

Christy: Go on, Lizzie.

Lizzie: I'm not telling you, Eliza Chase, so there.

Kathy: Come on, Lizzie Borden, what y'got to be ashamed of?

Lizzie: Nothin'.

Irma: So tell then.

Lizzie: No, I shan't.

Dorothy: We'll ask your Emma.

Lizzie: Don't care if you do.

Kathy: Yeah, your sister'll tell us.

Lizzie: No she won't . . . don't you pretend she will.

Irma: Aw come on, Lizzie – tell us.

Lizzie: And anyway, you don't know my sister.

Kathy: I do too.

Irma: Come on, Lizzie.

Eliza: You know my middle name.

Georgina: And mine.

Hortense: Mine too.

Irma: And Kathy's.

Jo: And you said you would.

Lizzie: No I never did.

Irma: You did too.

Lizzie: I never said . . . you just thought I did.

Ann: You tell lies, Lizzie Borden.

Barbara: You make things up.

(*Main stage lights dim, spotlight on Lizzie. The rest of the cast freeze.*)

Lizzie: 'Mrs Borden told me she had had a note and was going out. She said she would get the dinner. She did not tell me when she was coming back. I did not know. I had no occasion to use the axe or hatchet. I knew there was an old axe downstairs and last time I saw it, it was on the old chopping-block. I don't know whether my father owned a hatchet or not. Assuming a hatchet was found in the cellar I don't know how it got there.'

(*Main stage lights back up, spotlight out. Break the freeze.*)

Barbara: You always make up your own rules.

Dorothy: Every game we play.

Lizzie: That's not true.

Irma: Anyhow why won't you tell? Eh?

Kathy: It's only a name.

Lizzie: So . . . .

May: I know it begins with an 'A'.

Lizzie: You keep quiet now!

(*The others form a half-circle around Lizzie.*)

Irma: Lizzie Annabel.

Lizzie: No!

Dorothy: Lizzie Abigail.

Lizzie: No – not that!

Kathy: Lizzie Arethusa.

May: Agamemnon.

Barbara: Agatha.

Frances: Anastasia.

Lizzie: No! No! No! Stop it now!

Rachel (*A small girl hugging a doll and frightened of Lizzie*): I know her name.

Lizzie: You keep quiet, Rachel Brayton – you go play with your dolls.

All: Tell us then, Rache.
Come on, Rache.
Don't mind her.
(*Ad lib.*)

Lizzie: *Don't you dare tell.*

Ann: Pay no heed, Rachel, you tell us.

Lizzie: I'm warning you – just you tell and you'll be sorry.

Irma: Come on, Rache . . . . .

Rachel: It's . . . . .

Lizzie: Rachel! (*Snatches her doll.*)

Rachel: I won't tell, Lizzie, honest I won't . . . give it back.

Lizzie: Well, you just remember, that's all. No telling! Or else . . .

(*Rachel quickly takes the doll back, and hugs it.*)

Christy: You're a bully, Lizzie.

Dorothy: Always wanting your own way.

Christy: We always get to do what you want.

(*Main stage lights dim, spotlight on Jo. The rest of the cast freeze.*)

Jo: 'On Thursday, August 4, 1892, I arose at 6.15 dressed and went downstairs. I always got up at this time ever since I was employed by the Bordens. I went to the cellar and brought up firewood and lit the stove. Miss Lizzie told me what to get for breakfast and when to clear away. She also said that I should wash the windows while Mrs Borden was dusting inside.'

(*Stage lights back up, spotlight out. Break the freeze.*)

Barbara: Ordering us about.

Dorothy: Just like we was your servants or something.

Ann: Always hollerin' and hollerin'.

(*Main stage lights dim, spotlight on May. The rest of the cast freeze.*)

May: 'Then I went up to my room and laid in my bed. The next sound I heard was the City Hall bell ringing eleven o'clock.'

(*Ann takes over the place in the spotlight from May.*)

Ann: 'I went to the store at about eleven o'clock. The store was right in the next street. I was not there long. I bought some groceries for dinner and returned to my home. I saw Bridget Sullivan going across the street to Dr Bowen's. She looked very white. I thought someone was sick. She was running. I went home and in through the back door. I then looked out of the window and I saw Lizzie on the inside of their screen door – she seemed excited – but not sad – more excited and I asked her if she was all right. She answered.'

(*Lizzie moves into spotlight.*)

Lizzie: 'Bridget come down quick. Father's dead!
Somebody came in and killed him.
Oh, do come over, please. Someone has killed Father!

(*Stage lights back up, spotlight out. Break the freeze.*)

(*Lizzie runs off stage left.*)

Lizzie (*As she goes*): Leave me alone, all of you!!

Hortense (*Says or sings, wistfully*):
Lizzie Borden took an axe
And gave her mother forty whacks.
When she saw what she had done
She gave her father forty-one.

Barbara (*To Georgina*): What you got there?

Georgina: Lizzie Borden dropped it.

(*The children gather round Georgina.*)

Ann: What is it?

Eliza: Prayer book it looks like.

Barbara: Sure it's hers?

Frances: Look for the name.

Irma: Yeah, it's hers all right – there's her name in it.
. . . Hey – look see – it's her *full* name.
Lizzie *Andrew* Borden.

Ann: Andrew?

Christy: But that's a boy's name.

Ann: Don't I know it.

Barbara: What's she doing with a boy's name?

Irma: Andrew!

Jo: Could have been worse – could have been Albert.

Irma: Andrew Borden! What a name for a girl.

Ann: She's as strong as a boy.

Barbara: She's as strong as a horse.

Dorothy: She looks like one too! (*Laughs*)

Kathy: You see her fight last week – she sure is tough.

May: Almost kill you she could . . . if she felt like it.

(*Lizzie re-enters from left. There is a pause; Lizzie is aware of something wrong.*)

Irma: Hey Lizzie – we know your middle name.

All (*Chant, taunting her*):
We know your name.
We know your name.
We know your name.

Lizzie: You stop it!

Irma: Andrew! Andrew! Andrew!

Lizzie: Stop it, I tell you.

Ann: Did your parents want a boy?

Barbara: Yeah, that must be it.

Irma: Good thing they didn't want a dog –

Barbara: . . . they'd've called her Rover!

(*Laughs, whistles, barks.*)

Lizzie: Rachel Brayton, I warned you.

Rachel: Wasn't me that told, Lizzie – honest! (*She hides her doll behind her back.*)

Lizzie: It's all your fault – I won't forget – you'll suffer.

Christy: It was in your book, Lizzie.

Lizzie: Give it here.

(*They offer the book back to Lizzie, and she snatches it.*)

Stealin' other folks' things.

Georgina: We found it, honest.

Christy: Just lying there.

(*Main stage lights dim, spotlight on Eliza. The rest of the cast freeze.*)

Eliza: 'I went into the sitting room and saw the form of Mr Borden lying on the sofa. His face was very badly cut with apparently a sharp instrument. There was blood all over his face; his face was covered in blood. I felt his pulse and satisfied myself he was dead, and took a glance about the room and saw that nothing was disturbed at all. The body was lying with its face toward the right side, apparently at ease, as anyone would if they were asleep. I could hardly recognise the face.'

(*Stage lights back up, spotlight out. Break the freeze slowly.*)

All (*A whisper at first, becoming stronger.*):
'Lizzie Borden took an axe
And gave her mother forty whacks
Then she stood behind the door
And gave her father forty more.'

(*This becomes a skipping game, as they jump in and out of a long rope.*)

'Matthew, Mark, Luke and John
Next door neighbour carry on.'

(*The game continues during the dialogue – the words might even be spoken like a skipping rhyme, in rhythm with the rope.*)

Christy: C'mon, Lizzie, you can join in.

Ann: No, she can't.

Christy: Why not?

Irma: 'Cos we don't have boys playing skipping games.

(*Lizzie storms off left again.*)

Christy: Lizzie ain't a boy.

Jo: She's got a boy's name.

Irma: Sure has – she's called Andrew.

Christy: All the same she's a girl.

Christy: }
Georgina: } Sticks and stones may break my bones
But names and such won't hurt me!

Ann: }
Barbara: }
Irma: } Slugs and snails and puppy-dog's tails
Jo: } That's what little boys are made of.
Kathy: }

Ann: Andrew Borden – some girl's name –

Christy: She can't help her name nohow.

Barbara: What sort o' name's that, for heaven's sakes?

Christy: Leave off now – she can't help it.

Ann:
Barbara: } What you say? Just what you say?

Christy: } I said she can't help it.
Georgina: } She cain't help it.

(*The rope stops. The main stage lights dim, spotlight on Dorothy. The rest of the cast freeze.*)

Dorothy: 'Soon after Miss Russell arrived Lizzie said she wished someone would try to find Mrs Borden for she thought she had heard her come in. Bridget and I started to go to find her, we went through the dining-room, out of the sitting-room where Mr Borden's body was lying and into the hall. As I went upstairs I turned my head to the left, and as I got up to where my eyes were on a level with the landing I could see into the guest room. At the far side of the room I saw something that looked like the form of a person.'

(*The rope starts, the cast all chant the skipping rhyme in rhythm with the rope.*)

All: 'Not last night, the night before
24 robbers came knocking at my door
As I went out to let them in
This is what they said to me . . .

(*Kathy replaces Dorothy in the spotlight. The rope stops.*)

Kathy: 'I saw Mrs Borden laid down between the bed and the dressing-table, face downward with her head all broke in or cut and she was dead. In the room and near the body I noticed blood spots. The body was laying in a pool of blood, and there was blood upon the pillow cases and the dressing-table.'

(*Main stage lights back up, spotlight out. Break the freeze, collect in the rope.*)

(*Lizzie re-enters with a bunch of wild flowers from the left.*)

Eliza: Hey, look, it's Lizzie!

Frances: What yer doin' now, Lizzie?

May: What'you playin'?

Frances: What ye got the flowers for?

Christy: Can we play, Lizzie?

Georgina: What is it, Lizzie?

Lizzie: It's called 'Funerals'.

Hortense: What's that mean?

Christy: Buryin' folk, that's what it is.

Ann: Some game.

Lizzie: Don't cha wanna play?

Georgina: How d'we do it, Lizzie?

Lizzie: It's buryin' folk.

Hortense: Buryin'?

Lizzie: When they're all dead and finished and no use no more . . .

Frances: You shouldn't speak o' such things, Lizzie.

May: 'Tain't decent.

Lizzie: 'Tis so!

May (*Superior*): My mother says you shouldn't even talk about such things.

Lizzie: Well then, I reckon your ma must be silly – I reckon.

May: Well, at least she's my *real* ma, ain't no steppin-mother.

Ann: Leave off, May. Tell us about funerals, Lizzie.

Georgina: What the flowers for, Lizzie?

Dorothy: Allus has flowers at a funeral.

Barbara: No – that's a wedding.

Lizzie: Y'have flowers at 'em both, I reckon.

Barbara: I seen 'em at weddings.

Hortense: I was a bridesmaid once – I think.

Ann: So've I been – lots o' times.

Irma: You haven't so – you're only making it up.

Ann: I meant funerals.

Lizzie: Well that's not true neither, and I know things for certain, 'cos my pa's a mortician.

Christy: A what, Lizzie?

Lizzie: A mortician – he buries people.

May: Where?

Lizzie: In the ground – at the churchyard.

Hortense: That's spooky, I reckon.

Lizzie: In coffins –

May: I'm scared.

Lizzie: And he embalms 'em too . . .

All: What's that mean?
Tell us about that, Lizzie.
Yeah, tell us. } (*Ad lib.*)

(*Again they gather round Lizzie. She has their attention.*)

Lizzie: Why it's preservin' the body – that's what it is.

Ann: Preservin'?

Barbara: What fer?

Hortense: Yer mean like bottlin' fruit?

Georgina: How d'he do it, Lizzie?

Irma: Have you seen him?

Jo: Have you watched him?

Lizzie: Course I have – many times . . . and I've *helped* him.

All: No!
You ain't!
(etc.) } (*Ad lib.*)

Ann: You're makin' it up.

All: What's he do then?
How's he do it? } (*Ad lib.*)

Lizzie: Well, he uses all kind o' things . . . like . . . hot wax . . .

All (*A whisper*): Hot wax?

Lizzie: . . . and thick brown varnish . . .

All (*Louder*): Thick brown varnish?

Lizzie: . . . and lots of wrapping cloth.

All (*Even louder*): Wrapping cloth?

Ann (*Scathingly*): She's makin' it all up.

Lizzie: Don't cha wanna hear, then?

All: Yeah . . . tell us.
Carry on.
Go on, Lizzie. } (*Ad lib.*)

Lizzie: No, I ain't gonna . . .

All: Aw!

Lizzie: We'll play funerals first, then I'll tell you.

Kathy: Well, who's gonna be dead?

All: Me . . . me . . . me . . .
Let me.
I wanna.
Not me.
(*Ad lib.*)

Christy: You choose, Lizzie.

Lizzie: Lemme see then . . . keep quiet, lemme pick . . . Rachel Brayton!

Rachel: No! Lizzie! Not me . . . I don' wanna be dead.

Barbara: Aw c'mon Rache . . . won't hurt none.

May: You be dead first, then someone else can have a turn.

Rachel: I don' wanna . . . I'm scared . . .

Kathy: What you gotta be scared of?

Irma: Someone's gotta be dead.

Jo: Yeah.

Lizzie: Tell you what . . . we'll use your doll, Rache . . . that way you can be the chief mourner.

Rachel: No! No! (*Rachel's protests are drowned in the agreement of the others.*)

Lizzie: Now we all need flowers. Rachel, you c'n have these. And we need a hymn. You get the flowers and sing . . . I'll get the coffin . . . sing!

(*Lizzie goes off stage left. Rachel remains crying and holding the flowers centre. The rest move about the edges of the stage 'picking' imaginary flowers and singing.*)

All (Sing):
All things bright and beautiful

All creatures great and small
All things wise and wonderful
The Lord God made them all.

He gave us eyes to see them
And lips that we might tell
How great is God Almighty
Who has made all things well.

All things bright and beautiful
All creatures great and small
All things wise and wonderful
The Lord God made them all.

(*During the last chorus they form up as a congregation in a church, with Rachel, still crying, at the front. Lizzie re-enters, draped in a veil and cloak, bearing a cardboard box – the 'congregation' hum the hymn chorus again.*)

(*Lizzie takes up a position with her back to the audience.*)

Lizzie: Dearly beloved, we are here today to bid farewell to the remains of our friend.

Hortense: Amen.

Lizzie: Not yet! I'll tell you when. Taken from us so suddenly and unexpectedly . . . now we're here to bury it . . . earth to earth and ashes to ashes and dust to dust.

(*Rachel's crying becomes louder.*)

We'll now say the Lord's prayer . . .
Our Father . . .

All: . . . which are in heaven
Hallowed be Thy name,
Thy kingdom . . .

(*They tail off as there is a realisation that they may be doing wrong – only Lizzie continues; the others back away from her.*)

Lizzie: Thy will be done in earth as it
is in Heaven,
Give us this day our daily bread
And forgive us our trespasses . . .

Rachel (*Screams*): No!

(*She rushes to Lizzie and snatches the box and opens it – she screams and takes out a very broken doll, clothing torn and the head broken – and arm and leg missing*.)

Lizzie: . . . as we . . . forgive . . . them . . . that . . .
trespass . . . against . . . us.

(*Lizzie turns on this and lifts her veil and drops her cloak – she is spattered with blood all over her face, apron and hands*.)

(*The lights change to blues. The cast sing*.)

All: Yesterday in old Fall River
Mr Andrew Borden died.
Now they've got his daughter Lizzie
On a charge of homicide
Some folks say she didn't do it
Others say of course she did
But they all admit she was a very funny sort of kid.

Chorus
Oh you can't chop your momma up in Massachusetts
And then go out and blame it on the mice – oh no.
And you can't chop your poppa up in Massachusetts
You know your friends are bound to criticise.

(*The chorus is sung again and a square dance chain develops round Lizzie and Rachel, who hold their positions*.)

CURTAIN

Drama ideas

1 Select a page or half a page of the script and try to improvise the dialogue while playing a game of 'tag' or 'hop-scotch' or some similar playground game.

2 Improvise the scene that is related in the script by Frances/Francis concerning Mrs Borden's cat. How might you achieve the appropriate and horrific effect of the discovery of the cat?

3 Work in twos or threes. Imagine that Rachel's doll was not only precious to her, but was perhaps new. Explore the scene on her return home from school in which she has to explain the breaking of it to her parents.

4 Work with a partner. Imagine that one of you is a neighbour of the Borden family, and the other is someone who is visiting Fall River. What can the neighbour tell the visitor about the Borden family?

If the neighbour was interviewed by the press, would he or she be prepared to speak so freely? Reverse your previous roles and try out this interview.

5 Work in a group of two or three. Imagine that it is many years after the murders, and that Lizzie is now a very old woman and close to death. One of you is Lizzie and the others are friends of hers from the town – perhaps one is the local preacher. Is it possible, at this late stage, to persuade Lizzie to tell the real truth of what happened so long ago?

Follow-up work

1 Make your own collection of what might be considered to be cruel or violent events in well-known nursery rhymes and 'fairy' stories.

2 The public attitude to the 'Fall River Murders' changed remarkably rapidly. Initially it was against Lizzie Borden, then it swung to the opposite extreme during the trial, with a great deal of sympathy being shown towards Lizzie; and then after her acquittal a strong doubt grew as to whether justice had really been done.

How might a newspaper reporter in 1892 have reflected these attitudes – what headlines might he have written, and what would have been his first paragraph on each occasion?

‘I was a Good Little Girl ’til . . .’

Introduction

The name 'Suffragettes' is applied to the group of women, from all classes of society, who campaigned between 1903 and 1914 to secure 'votes for women'. Their name comes from the word 'suffrage', which means the right to vote.

Today the women's movement has progressed to campaigning for equal opportunities in all areas of employment. Nowadays there may be female doctors, female lawyers, female jockeys and female government ministers, all of which positions would have been far less accessible a generation ago. And it was first securing the right to vote which represented a major step towards wider opportunities in employment and society as a whole.

Although the principle of 'votes for women' began to be mentioned as early as 1825, it was a long time before any noticeable action could be taken to achieve it. In the 1850s there came a change in the Victorian attitude to women. One reason for this was the work of Florence Nightingale, whose impact on the standards of nursing during the Crimean War demonstrated that it was possible for women to establish their own careers and responsible places in society. From this realisation came increasing demands for extending the franchise, or right to vote at public elections. Not all men had the right to vote at this time, so that the suggestion that women might obtain this right was still quite radical.

The Suffragette movement in Great Britain is linked directly with the name of Emmeline Pankhurst, who, together with her daughters Christabel and Sylvia, led many of the battles between 1903 and 1914 that brought the cause of women's suffrage to the notice of the whole country, if not the whole world.

Starting in Manchester, the movement grew rapidly, gaining supporters from all walks of life – from the upper class to the working class and both men and women.

Led by the Pankhursts and others who identified themselves with the cause, the Suffragettes began a campaign of civil disobedience to draw attention to their demands. What began with chalking slogans on pavements, chaining themselves to railings in prominent places, and breaking windows, became protest marches and meetings, setting fire to pillar boxes and damaging public property. Emily Davidson, who died after throwing herself under the hooves of the King's horse in the middle of a race, was regarded as a martyr to the cause.

There were many arrests and many Suffragettes went to prison for their beliefs. In prison, many of the women continued to protest by starting hunger-strikes. The government dealt with these hunger-strikers most callously and cruelly by force-feeding them, and then by the introduction of the 'Cat and Mouse' Act, whereby a Suffragette who became too weak in prison through hunger-strikes and ill-treatment was released only to be imprisoned once she was well again. The health of many of the women was ruined by this treatment. But the intensity of the campaign showed the determination of women to achieve their rights.

With the outbreak of the First World War the campaign halted. The Suffragette prisoners were released, and the women proved their worth by taking on responsible jobs for the war effort. Many drove lorries and ambulances and worked in factories. Others took over the jobs of men who were fighting at the front. As a direct result of the part that women played in the First World War – and perhaps the memory of the strength of their Suffragette campaign before then – women were finally given the vote in December 1917. At first only women over thirty were allowed to vote; it was 1928 before the vote was extended to all women on the same basis as for men.

Great Britain was behind all these countries in giving women the vote: Australia (1902), Denmark (1915), Finland (1906), Iceland (1915), New Zealand (1893) and Russia (1917).

Lady Constance Lytton was a dedicated follower of Mrs Pankhurst. She had already been to prison for her beliefs, and was convinced that working-class women were being more harshly treated than those of higher social standing. To prove her point, and although she had a serious heart disease, she took the risk of disguising herself as 'Jane Warton', an ordinary working woman, and suffered arrest.

Her long hair had been cut, spectacles changed her looks, her clothing had been bought with a careful eye to effect; the matron and wardresses suspected nothing. Prison dress now replaced her 'Jane Warton' disguise. She announced her adoption of the hunger-strike. She was asked the usual medical questions which she refused to answer except to say that she was not suffering from any infectious disease. She was prepared, however, to submit to a medical examination of her heart, had it been suggested. It was not suggested. This had been precisely her policy when, as Lady Constance Lytton, she was imprisoned at Newcastle. Next day the senior medical officer appeared, but he asked her no questions and made no examination. All meals were brought to her cell but she ate nothing. Her bedding was removed from the cell during the day as she would not roll it up but lay on it in the day-time – a very wise proceeding on her part. On the fourth day of her imprisonment she was informed that forcible feeding would be employed; she replied that when legislators ceased to resist enfranchising women, she would cease to resist taking food. A few hours later the medical officer arrived in her cell, with four or five wardresses and the feeding apparatus.

No examination was made of her pulse and heart. As Lady Constance Lytton, she had had a heart examination by two prison doctors and another who, as it seemed, had come from London, and as a result was not forcibly fed, but released. As 'Jane Warton', the working woman, she had no heart examination at all, and was forcibly fed. Four wardresses held her down, a fifth helped in the forcible feeding process. The doctor offered the choice of a steel or a wooden gag, explaining that the steel gag would hurt. The prisoner was silent. After an effort with the wooden gag, the steel gag was used. Her jaws were forced painfully wide, the large tube pushed far down her throat and food very quickly poured down but returned in a few seconds after, in a bout of sickness, while doctor and wardresses held down her retching body. Then they left – no clean clothing could then be supplied, it seemed, and she lay as she was, until the next morning. From the next cell the distressing sounds of the forcible feeding of Elsie Howey could be heard.

The following day, Lady Constance was fed by force a second time. The suffering and the sickness were this time worse than before. The same evening doctors and wardresses came again to the cell. Again the horror and the vomiting and now while the vomiting continued, so did the inpouring of food. After this third feeding Lady Constance showed greater signs of illness than before and the doctor called in the assistant medical officer, who happened to be nearby, to test her heart. He rapidly did so and cheerfully pronounced it a 'splendid heart', but his senior seemed less confident. The fourth time, the doctor brought brandy and Bovril with his feeding contrivance, but afterward the sufferer felt a reaction of intense cold. Next morning, the same food as at first was used and again came the sickness. At last, one morning, the Governor and doctor arrived together at her cell door. It was to tell her that she was released on medical grounds. Her sister, Lady Emily Lutyens, had come to take her home. The Press Association had heard a rumour that she was a prisoner in Walton Gaol. The prison officials had informed the Prison Commissioners in London that their mysterious prisoner was, they suspected, someone other than she professed to be.

Lady Constance had proved her point: that the Liberal Government had, as she pointed out in a letter to the Home Secretary, a different standard of treatment for working women and for other women. When she was Lady Constance Lytton, they found her to be suffering from serious valvular disease of the heart and unfit for forcible feeding. When she was 'Jane Warton', they did not even question the state of her heart and fed her by force.

Lady Constance had made a stand for real democracy. She had taken a desperate risk for votes for women.

Staging the play

The action of the play in performance must flow easily from one scene into the next. Try to imagine an Edwardian street scene, peopled with characters from all classes and all walks of life, who at times group together to discuss the activities of the Suffragettes and at other times act out scenes from the militant campaign. This should achieve the necessary 'ensemble' effect in the acting. It would be most effective if the performers only went offstage for vital costume changes or for the setting and striking of properties, so that the 'busy' effect on stage, and even in the auditorium, can be maintained throughout.

In order to achieve the various scenes required in this play, and give opportunities for grouping the characters well, you may find it an advantage to have a higher level at the rear of the stage with steps down to the front area. This should give a good basis for the 'street scenes' that punctuate the action of the documentary. At other times the area has to represent a prison, a chapel, the House of Commons, a courtroom, etc. and you will need to consider what properties need to be added to create the scenes with the minimum of effort – possibly being set and struck by the cast. So, for example, some 'iron' railings used in the street scene might be moved to create a dock in the courtroom, and a high level for the judge in the same scene become a pulpit area for the chaplain: try to use as many of these 'doublings' of the use of properties as you can. For the force-feeding scene, perhaps a shadowgraph effect could be used. For this you need a screen made of a sheet or similar cloth held taut with a bright light behind. The performers then act between the light source and the screen so that all action is seen in silhouette. Try some experiments with this effect. The positioning of the performers is very important in achieving a good and understandable effect.

With the costuming of the play try to suggest the Edwardian period as fully as possible. This need not create too many problems for basic costumes. The girls can wear a long skirt and a high-necked blouse while the boys could have dark trousers, a plain shirt and a waistcoat. ('Jeans' are out of period and ought not therefore to be used.) To the basic outfits try to add extra items to suggest the individual characters, so that the richer 'ladies' might have elaborate hats, rich shawls or feather boas, or parasols, the poorer might have aprons and shawls, or scarves and mittens. If you can obtain top hats, bowler hats, frock coats or tailcoats to add character to the boys this would help tremendously. Similarly there is an advantage in being able to suggest prison dress easily – possibly through the use of aprons overprinted with large prison arrows. Helmets for the policemen would be a great help too. Do remember, however, that provided the character is well presented in voice and manner by the actor or actress the audience will generally accept some inaccuracies in costume.

Many characters are presented quite briefly and therefore try to establish them as strongly as possible, using as wide a range of voices as your group can manage. Several of the longer speeches are taken directly from what the characters actually did say.

The sound effects that are necessary can probably be organised most satisfactorily by the cast. There would be a distinct advantage to having a barrel organ on stage for setting the atmosphere, or such an effect available through a speaker system. The songs could be sung unaccompanied which would be very impressive, or 'street' musicians could be introduced to make the music a part of the whole 'street' presentation. Certainly any such musicians should feel free to move about the auditorium both before and during the performance.

Apart from the shadowgraph scene there is no need to have any elaborate lighting. However, some directors might wish to spotlight specific characters, or groups of characters and certainly this can help in focusing the audience's attention. If you have access to a good lighting set-up, it is worth remembering that lights that are directed across the stage can create some extremely good effects.

'I was a Good Little Girl 'til . . .'

The characters

Newsboy
Lady Bagot
Lady Amberley
Lady Combermore } Wealthy ladies
Mrs Thompson
Mrs Russell
Mrs Parkes } Middle-class women
Mrs Fearnley
Mrs Murray
Mr Murray } Very much upper middle-class
Ethel
Kathleen
Annie } Working-class women
Mrs Emmeline Pankhurst
1st Heckler
2nd Heckler
3rd Heckler
4th Heckler
5th Heckler
Mr William Cremer, MP
Girl
Policeman
Postman
Mr H. H. Asquith, the Prime Minister
Magistrate
A wealthy man
Ponsonby, aide to the King
Mr Masterman, MP
Wardress
Governor
Mary Leigh, a Suffragette
Prison Chaplain

The first performance by the Dewsbury Arts Group (Youth section)

Mr Keir Hardie, MP
Newsgirl
'General' Flora Drummond
Narrator
Other Newsgirls, Suffragettes, Warders and Wardresses.

The sound of a barrel organ is heard and, as the curtain opens, we see an Edwardian street scene, characters move onto the scene from both the wings and the auditorium. There is general street business and ad libs to set the period – street games, and traders bustling about and shouting their wares. A Newsboy runs about the stage and possibly the auditorium selling his papers and shouting.

Newsboy: Resignation of Mr Balfour! Conservatives defeated at general election! Read all about it!

(*A group of ladies are overheard talking, stage right – Ladies Amberley, Bagot and Combermore.*)

Lady Bagot: It's not the Conservatives that worry me – nor the Liberals bless their hearts. It's this woman Pankhurst with all her liberal ideas and I mean that in the worst sense.

Lady Amberley: She's from Manchester, I believe.

Lady Bagot: That's correct – in Lancashire, so they say.

Lady Amberley: And yet apparently educated.

Lady Bagot: I believe so. She actually held a public appointment there – as Registrar of Births and Deaths.

Lady Amberley: No!

Lady Bagot: And her daughter is studying for a degree of some kind.

Lady Amberley: Really? What are those northerners thinking of?

Lady Bagot: Quite my dear – one sometimes wonders about the behaviour of the provinces.

(*Another group is overheard, stage left: these women are middle-class – Mrs Thompson, Mrs Russell and Mrs Parkes.*)

Mrs Thompson: It's her family I feel sorry for.

Mrs Russell: Four children to support.

Mrs Parkes: And her husband dead.

Mrs Russell: Poor thing.

Mrs Thompson: Mind you, she ought to know better, behaving the way she does.

Mrs Parkes: And encouraging others.

Mrs Russell: She's one of those politicals.

Mrs Thompson: Not a Bolshevik?

Mrs Parkes: Don't say that.

Mrs Russell: A Socialist, I believe.

Mrs Thompson: They count as Bolsheviks! She deserves all she gets.

(*The Newsboy runs about the stage again, selling papers.*)

Newsboy: The Votes for Women Bill fails to be introduced. Government talk out vote proposals.

(*Another group is overheard, at rear stage right: they are upper middle-class – Mrs Fearnley, Mr and Mrs Murray.*)

Mrs Fearnley: It's all the Government's fault.

Mrs Murray: Nonsense. Absolute stuff and nonsense. My husband says so – don't you, George?

Mr Murray (*Reading his newspaper*): Hmph!

Mrs Fearnley: I tell you, my dear, it is entirely the Government's doing. The idea of giving all adults the vote is not new.

Mrs Murray: Then why blame this Government?

Mrs Fearnley: Because the Liberals are at the moment concerned with stopping all bills that might extend the vote – especially to women.

Mr Murray (*Reading his newspaper*): Hmph!

Mrs Murray: Really? I didn't know that – I'll never trust that nice Mr Balfour again.

Mrs Fearnley: It's not him now dear – he was a Conservative. It's Sir Henry Campbell-Bannerman – he's the Liberal man.

Mrs Murray: I really can't keep track of them all, they do seem to come and go so quickly. Whatever happened to Mr Disraeli?

Mr Murray (*Lowering his paper and talking directly to the audience*): Votes for women indeed! We shall be asked next to give votes to horses and dogs!

(*A fourth group is overheard, at rear stage left: they are working-class – Ethel, Kathleen and Annie.*)

Ethel: It's all very well for the likes of 'er – she's somebody, she is.

Kathleen: She'll never have to worry about where the next penny's coming from.

Ethel: 'Ere, can you lend me two pence 'til Friday – I've got nuffin' to give the kids.

Kathleen: Blimey! Yo're askin' a lot – I've 'ad to pawn the Sunday clo'es agin this week.

Annie: We get eighteen shillin's a week – an' it goes nowhere.

Ethel: Husbands don't know how much fings cost and that's a fact!

Kathleen: We don't get a bloomin' livin' – we get an existence. Ever since my old man died, *I* do all the work; *I* keep the 'ome – I reckon I ought to have a vote for it.

(*Mrs Pankhurst appears stage left and moves to a position centre rear, top level. An Assistant with her gives out pamphlets.*)

Annie: That's what she's always going on about.

Ethel: Who?

Kathleen: Mrs Pankhurst.

(*As Mrs Pankhurst speaks, the cast forms a crowd around her.*)

Mrs Pankhurst: Votes for Women! Votes for Women! That is what we ask the Government for. This is not a new idea – not a new plea – indeed the movement to give women the vote goes back over seventy-five years . . .

1st Heckler: *I'm* not old enough to remember that far back!

(*Laughter.*)

Mrs Pankhurst: It is a movement that has been beset by procrastination – Government procrastination!

2nd Heckler: 'Ere watch yor language, there may be some ladies present.

(*More laughter.*)

Mrs Pankhurst: Time and time again we have been told to wait, that the necessary legislation would come. We have waited. And still there is no answer. How much longer must we wait?

3rd Heckler: As long as the train's standing in the station!

(*More laughter.*)

Mrs Pankhurst: Sir Edward Grey was asked at a public meeting, 'Will the Liberal Government give votes to women?' – he avoided replying. Mr Winston Churchill . . .

4th Heckler: Who's 'e when 'e's at 'ome?

Mrs Pankhurst: Mr Winston Churchill, standing as a prospective Liberal candidate was asked – 'If you are elected, will you make women's suffrage a Government measure?'

5th Heckler: Let 'em suffer away *I* say!

Mrs Pankhurst: *I* say we have now waited long enough. The Women's Social and Political Union now says 'Deeds not Words', 'Rise up Women' – we shall not rest until the vote is ours. Too long have we been pacified, been patient, *and been ignored*! Now we shall make our presence felt.

(*Some applause and cheering.*)

Mrs Pankhurst (*Moving forward to the front of the stage and directing her song at cast and audience alike, she sings*):
Fall in and follow me! Fall in and follow me!
Come along and never mind the weather,
All together, stand *by* me *girls*;
I know the way to go, I'll take you for a spree;
You do as I do, and you'll do right,
Fall in, and follow me.

Kathleen: It's high time some real action was taken.

All (*Sing*):
Fall in and follow me! Fall in and follow me!
Come along and never mind the weather,
All together, stand by *us* girls;
We know the way to go, we'll take you for a spree;
You do as we do, and you'll do right,
Fall in and follow me!

(*During the singing of the chorus, a dance might be introduced in which Lady Combermore, Mrs Parkes, Mrs Fearnley and Annie 'join' Mrs Pankhurst. Others might refuse. The chorus could be repeated to achieve this effect if necessary. At the end the crowd applaud themselves and then sit across the rear of the stage, each holding their pamphlet as though it were an order sheet in the House of Commons. Mr Cremer steps forward stage left.*)

Mr Cremer: I have always contended that if once we open the door, and give the vote to even a small number of females, then we cannot ever possibly close it – and it will mean ultimately complete adult suffrage – the vote for everyone! Is this what the Government wants?

All (*as MPs*) (*Lowering their order papers, ad. lib.*): No! Not at all! Shame! Disgraceful!

Mr Cremer: The Government of this great country would therefore be handed over to a majority who would not be men – but women!

All (*as MPs*) (*Lowering their order papers again, ad. lib.*): Shame! Horsewhip them!

Mr Cremer: Women are creatures of impulse and emotion and do not decide questions on the grounds of reason as men do.

Mrs Fearnley (*Stands*): Woman-hater!

Mr Cremer: I am indeed sometimes described as a woman-hater, yet may I point out that I have had *two* wives – that is surely the best answer that I can give to those who call me a woman-hater. Indeed I am too fond of women to see them dragged into the political arena, and to ask them to undertake responsibilities, duties and obligations, which they do not understand nor care for.

(*A restlessness grows in the crowd, murmurs as they lower their papers and stand – now becoming a restless crowd.*)

Mr Cremer: If you try to talk politics in the company of women, what happens?

Crowd (*Softly*): Votes for Women! Give us the vote!

Mr Cremer (*Some panic in his voice.*): I'll tell you what happens – you are soon asked to 'Stop talking silly politics'. Silly politics! I ask you! And we are being invited to hand over the destinies of the country to a type of people who think this way.

(*Crowd murmurs, objections and ad libs for the vote grow.*)

Mr Cremer (*Increasing in volume as crowd noise grows, he also backs away from them to centre stage.*): I ask you to pause and – er – consider most carefully before taking the – er – step suggested. I believe that if women are given the vote, it could mean disaster to all political parties. . . . Do not take a step from which you can never retreat.

(*He finds himself on the edge of the stage, with nowhere to go. The crowd noise grows and the order papers are crumpled to form stones to throw at him. Cremer is hit and falls to the ground. The crowd goes silent and moves to the edge of the stage, leaving one girl centre wearing a Suffragette sash and carrying a brick. Two men minister to Cremer and move him to the side of the stage, right.*)

Girl (*Sings*):

When I was young and innocent you came into my heart
You taught me things that I recall whenever we're apart
You taught me that the world was wide – but not too wide for me,
So now I'm just not satisfied with what I used to be.

I was a good little girl 'til I met you,
You set my head in a whirl my whole heart too,
Oh how you told me the tale – the way you do
I was a good little girl 'til I met you.

(*She is escorted off by one or two Policemen – she struggles violently all the way. Barrel organ music – and the crowd becomes a street scene again, with the groups in their original positions. Group one is overhead.*)

Lady Amberley: The men are quite right, of course – a woman's place is in the drawing-room.

Lady Bagot: Quite! It is a woman's duty to be decorative about the house.

Lady Combermore: You speak as though we were wallpaper. Decorative about the house indeed – you couldn't be more wrong. I went to a meeting and looked at, and sat among, a huge concourse of working women, who had met to demand the vote.

Lady Amberley: Working women? Really my dear!!

Lady Combermore: These women are the outcome of the Women's Social and Political Organisation. They have nothing to do with any of the old established suffrage societies, they meet under the Labour Party . . .

Lady Bagot: The Labour Party! Really, it makes me feel quite faint even to think about it!

Lady Combermore: They carry their own flags – they bring their children, carry their babies – poor infants – feeding them with lumps of cake . . .

Lady Amberley: *Cake*!! Good heavens, assuredly new winds are blowing through society. Whatever will they get up to next?

(*A mimed sequence, with barrel organ music underscoring , based on Suffragettes chaining themselves to railings. You could devise such a scene in improvisation work or use the idea of a Policeman on his beat who gradually notices an ever-increasing number of suffragettes chained to a length of railing. Eventually he thinks hard, blows his whistle and another Policeman enters. Together they take off the length of railing and the attached 'prisoners'. This scene could be applauded by some of the attendant crowd, and jeered by others. We overhear the second group again.*)

Mrs Thompson: It's you I feel sorry for.

Mrs Parkes: Why?

Mrs Russell: Going off with them Suffragettes.

Mrs Thompson: You ought to know better.

Mrs Parkes: But I agree with all they say and they're trying to make things better for all women.

Mrs Russell: Is that true? I thought they was political.

Mrs Parkes: They are – how else will they get anything done? (*She makes to leave*.)

Mrs Thompson: What are you up to now?

Mrs Parkes: I must go and chalk pavements for a meeting.

Mrs Thompson: A meeting?

Mrs Russell: Here, I'll come with you and chalk pavements too!

(*Mrs Parkes and Mrs Russell leave, stage left.*)

Mrs Thompson: 'Ere! (*But they've gone: she speaks to the audience.*) They're always up to something!

(*A character enters, carrying a sign '10 Downing Street' and stands centre rear. A Postman enters from stage left with Mrs Parkes and Mrs Russell with large luggage labels on them addressed to the Prime Minister. The Postman knocks on the address sign, a Policeman 'appears at the door'.*)

Policeman: Can I help you?

Postman: Special delivery. Recorded letters, sign here please.

Policeman: Oh very well. (*He signs.*) Now where are the letters?

Postman (*Indicating Suffragettes*): Here! (*He exits stage right.*)

Policeman: But . . . here, I say . . . this isn't on . . .

(*But the Postman has gone.*)

Policeman (*Looking at the labels*): To the Rt Hon. Herbert Henry Asquith, 10 Downing Street . . . Well, it does seem to be the correct address.

(*Mr Asquith enters from stage left to the Policeman.*)

Asquith: You have a problem, 84?

Policeman: Yes sir! These letters have just arrived for the Prime Minister. Will you take charge of them?

Asquith: Certainly not!

Policeman: But they are paid for, Sir.

Asquith (*To the Suffragettes*): You cannot be delivered here. You must be returned. As far as we are concerned you are dead letters.

(*He exits stage left followed by the Policeman. The Suffragettes move forward and sing to the audience.*)

Two Suffragettes (*Sing*):

Oh dear what can the matter be?
Asquith won't take us, it's part of his patter, he
Won't take a letter from Monday to Saturday
He won't accept the fe-male (mail!)

We're stamped, and we're paid for, our franking has been done,
We're sealed with a kiss, and the right address put on,
The postman has knocked, but the occupant stays dumb,
We're 'dead' but don't care to lie down.

All (*Joining in*):

Oh dear, what can the matter be?
Asquith won't take us, it's part of his patter, he
Won't take a letter from Monday to Saturday
He won't accept the fe-male (mail!)

(*A 'chain' dance in a straight line could be introduced on this chorus.*)

Newsboy (*Running about the stage and auditorium*):

Suffragettes stone Prime Minister.
Mr Asquith's Birmingham Visit attacked.
Government fails to stop militants.

(*The crowd move back into street scene and another group is overheard.*)

Mrs Fearnley: Every time there's a chance of change the Liberals stop it happening.

Mrs Murray: My husband says it's the Suffragettes' fault. Don't you, George?

Mr Murray (*Behind newspaper*): Hmph!

Mrs Fearnley: What about the way the Liberals stop all bills that might extend the vote?

Mrs Murray: Are they still doing that? What about that nice Mr Campbell-Bannerman, he said he'd help, I'm sure he did.

Mrs Fearnley: He's not Prime Minister any more – it's Mr Asquith now.

Mrs Murray: Oh yes – so it is! *Such* a trustworthy man.

Mrs Fearnley: You can't trust any of them – you mark my words.

Mrs Murray: I used to like that nice Mr Gladstone.

Mr Murray: Don't talk rubbish, Edith.

Mrs Fearnley: So – don't you think women are equal to men?

Mr Murray: Ha! Good Lord, no! – Why, woman was an afterthought.

Mrs Fearnley: Exactly! – and aren't second thoughts always best?

(*A Wealthy Man enters and buys a newspaper, front centre, from the Newsboy.*)

Wealthy Man: Good Lord! What a terrible score, the English cricket team has really gone to the bow-wows! Damned sport isn't what it was. Paper full of these Suffragette ninnies – want to get 'em all back in service. And what's this 'Explorer lost near Amazon'. Amazon? What's it all about, eh? You, boy, where is the Amazon?

Newsboy: She's in jail with the rest of 'em, I expect, guv. (*He moves to rear of stage.*)

(*The Wealthy Man remains on stage, at left, as we overhear yet another group.*)

Annie: I tell you she knows what she's on about.

Ethel: 'Ow can she? She's never done a stroke of real work in 'er life.

Kathleen: One of the toffs she is – plenty of money, I'll bet.

Annie: No she 'asn't – she works hard for the cause – she may not make brushes, or make shoes – but she works hard – and keeps a family, and pays into the Union funds.

Ethel: I reckon you're on 'er side then?

Annie: No – *she's* on *our* side! Just get that into your heads.

Kathleen: If we stick our necks out we could end up in jail.

Ethel: That's right – and then who looks after the kids?

Annie: The Union! And don't fret about jail – she doesn't – and she's been inside. And so have many others.

Kathleen: Blimey! Perhaps she means what she says!

(*Mrs Pankhurst moves forward stage right, with a 'dock' railing in front of her.*)

Mrs Pankhurst: You may wonder about the extremes to which we are prepared to go. Let me tell you that there is *no* limit. If we have to go to jail – we will go – but our protests will not end there. Prison will become another area of militant activities.

(*A Magistrate appears at centre on the top level.*)

Magistrate: This sort of thing shall come to an end, it must come to an end, I will bring it to an end. What have you to say?

Mrs Pankhurst: You have no authority to try women by laws made exclusively by men.

Magistrate: Two months imprisonment. What have you to say to that?

(*Other women join Mrs Pankhurst behind her 'dock'.*)

Mrs Pankhurst:
and Others: } Votes for Women!

Magistrate: Ten weeks! Take them away. Female hooligans!

(*The prisoners are moved off stage.*)

Newsboy (*Running about stage and auditorium*):
Arrest of 117 Suffragettes!
Five hours' raid on the Commons!
Prime Minister escapes unrecognised!
Black Rod's windows smashed!

Mr Murray (*Moving to left next to the Wealthy Man*):
Here, boy, I'll take a paper. (*He buys one.*)

Wealthy Man: Terrible news, isn't it?

Mr Murray: My wife is among them, Sir!

Wealthy Man: Good grief! I didn't realise – my condolences old man!

Mr Murray: Let me tell you, sir! I will subscribe ten pounds to the WSP Union for every day that my wife spends in prison. (*He exits stage right.*)

Wealthy Man (*To audience*): Ten pounds a day. Hm! – that seems a bargain – here, I say, do you think they'll take mine? (*He exits after Mr Murray stage right.*)

Newsboy (*Running about stage and auditorium*):
Women in goal!
Read all about it!
Suffragettes go on hunger strike.

(*He exits through auditorium. The Street Scene is re-formed. Ponsonby enters to centre rear.*)

Ponsonby: Marienbad: August 1909. His Majesty would be glad to know why the existing methods, which must obviously exist for dealing with prisoners who refuse nourishment, should not be adopted.

Masterman (*Entering front stage right*): House of Commons: September 1909. The State has a grave duty to these women. Their lives are sacred and must be preserved. Indeed the officials concerned would be liable for criminal proceedings if these prisoners were to commit suicide by starvation. Instead they have been 'induced' to take food, and there has been a progressive improvement in their health. Chains are not necessary under such hospital treatment; female wardresses do what has to be done under the supervision of the doctor.

(*The crowd move to allow a bench to be brought on and placed stage left for the cell. Mary Leigh enters from left and sits wearily. The crowd turn their backs on this scene.*)

Wardress (*Entering left*): Stand up for the Governor.

(*Mary Leigh stands, shakily, as the Governor enters from left.*)

Governor (*Pacing about*): Now then, eighteen, I've had a most unsatisfactory report about your behaviour. What have you to say about it?

(*During this interview, cast who are to be Prisoners leave the stage to put on prison aprons and caps.*)

Mary: Nothing . . . sir.

Governor: I'm told you have refused all food since your arrival.

Mary: That is correct.

Governor: You leave me little choice but to sentence you to nine days close confinement with bread and water. You will also lose forty-two days remission marks, and pay five shillings damage for the breaking of your cell windows.

Mary: I do not intend to pay any fine, nor do I intend to eat, nor obey any rules whilst I am imprisoned here.

Governor: You must listen carefully to what I have to say. I have orders from my superiors that you are not to be released even on medical grounds. If you still refrain from taking food I must order other measures to compel you to take it.

Mary: I refuse, and if you force food on me I want to know how you are going to do it.

Governor: That is a matter for me to decide.

Mary: I shall certainly hold you responsible, and shall take any measure in order to see whether you are justified in doing so.

Governor: Those are my orders. (*He exits stage left.*)

(*The Prison Chapel. Benches are set right and left by cast who are not involved in this scene. Then they exit. The Suffragette Prisoners walk in, in two lines from stage left and stage right.*)

Wardresses: }
Warders: } Tie up your cap string, twenty-seven. You look like a cinder-picker. You must learn to dress decently here.
Hold up your head, number thirty.
Hurry up, twenty-three.
Don't look about you, twelve.

(*When all are in place the Chaplain enters and takes up an elevated position stage right.*)

Chaplain: The General Epistle of James. Chapter 3. Verses 1–4. 'My brethren, be not many masters, knowing that we shall receive the greater condemnation. For in many things we offend all. If any man offend not in word, the same is a perfect man, and able also to bridle the whole body.

Behold, we put bits in the horses' mouths, that they may obey us; and we turn about their whole body.
Behold also the ships, which though they be so great, and are driven of fierce winds, yet are they turned about with a very small helm, withersoever the governor listeth.'
We will sing hymn number 371 – 'Father, hear the prayer we offer'.

Prisoners (*All sing*):
Father, hear the prayer we offer:
Not for ease that prayer shall be:
But for strength that we may ever
Live our lives courageously.

Not for ever in green pastures
Do we ask our way to be;
But the steep and rugged pathway
May we tread rejoicingly.

Not for ever by still waters
Would we idly rest and stay;
But would smite the living fountains
From the rocks along our way.

Be our strength in hours of weakness,
In our wanderings be our guide;
Through endeavour, failure, danger,
Father, be thou at our side.

(*During the singing of the hymn a mime of force-feeding is acted out on a shadowgraph. As the hymn ends we hear an ear-piercing scream from behind the shadowgraph screen and the lights go off. In the darkness the aprons and caps are removed, and the shadow screen.*)

Mr Keir Hardie (*Standing forward stage left: to audience*):
In reply to a question of mine today, Mr Masterman, speaking on behalf of the Home Secretary, admitted that some of the nine women prisoners now in Winson Green Gaol, Birmingham, had been subjected to 'hospital

treatment', and admitted that this euphemism meant administering food by force. The process employed was the insertion of a tube down the throat into the stomach and pumping the food down. To do this I am advised, a gag has to be used to keep the mouth open.

That there is difference of opinion concerning the tactics of the militant Suffragettes goes without saying, but surely there can be no two opinions concerning the horrible brutality of this proceeding? Women, worn and weak by hunger, are seized upon, held down by brute force, gagged, a tube inserted down the throat, or up the nostrils, and food poured or pumped into the stomach. Let British men think over the spectacle.

Mrs Pankhurst (*Moving to a position stage right forward: to audience sings*):
There is in Parliament today
One who tries to help the Suffragettes,
He aids them in their wordy fights,
For he thinks they ought to have their rights.
Votes! Votes! he wants for petticoats,
And if he could he'd surely have his way;
He strives for spinsters and for wives,
In fancy we can hear Keir Hardie say –

Mr Keir Hardie (*Turning to her*): Mrs Pankhurst . . .

All (*Sing*):
Put me amongst the girls!
Put me amongst the girls!
Do me a favour, do,
You know I'd do as much for you.
Put me amongst the girls,
Those with the curly curls;
They'll enjoy themselves, and so will I
If you put me amongst the girls.

(*The chorus could be sung by Keir Hardie initially with a reprise by the whole cast, or the chorus could be sung twice, gaining in volume and animation. Street scene again, the benches are removed. Banners and flags could be waved. Lady Bagot and Kathleen now actively involved.*)

Newsgirl (*Entering to front centre stage*): Read all about it! Government introduces 'Cat and Mouse' Act.

(*Newsboy enters – and sees that his 'pitch' has been taken – he stands next to Newsgirl . . . they shout as newspaper-sellers.*)

Newsboy: You've pinched me pitch!!

Newsgirl: That's just hard lines!!

Newsboy: I'll tell the coppers!!

Newsgirl: Votes for women!

(*She chases Newsboy off with a rolled up newspaper through the audience. The Wealthy Man enters from right, with a newspaper, to centre stage: he talks to the audience.*)

Wealthy Man: Quite a good wheeze, what! I mean full marks to the Home Secretary and all that. Damn good idea I reckon. Can't keep these fillies in jug all the time, hunger-striking and getting the country a bad name. When they become too weak, release 'em – then when they're fit again – y'can re-arrest them. Damn good idea, I say! Damn good idea!

(*Wealthy Man moves off stage left.*)

Lady Amberley: We cannot possibly let them die.

Mrs Thompson: It's them that I feel sorry for – all me friends that are in gaol.

Mrs Fearnley: Releasing them is the only sensible thing – as long as they're re-arrested of course.

Ethel: This 'ere Act is only to 'elp the upper classes – starvin's new to them – it isn't to us!

(Six chairs are brought on and placed in a row at front of stage. A bell rings and six Suffragette Prisoners enter and sit down, escorted by two Wardresses. A second bell rings and barrel organ music begins – the Prisoners get up and walk round the chairs, like 'musical chairs'. A bell rings a third time, and as the music stops, the chairs are rushed to, but one Prisoner collapses and is carried off. The process is repeated, and another collapses and is carried off. The crowd remaining clap in time with the music, stopping when the music stops. After the sixth prisoner is carried off, they all return and the crowd applauds. Street scene again, Wealthy Man returns, from stage left.)

Wealthy Man (*To audience*): And still those blessed women won't be good.

Lady Amberley: It's all in their breeding.

Wealthy Man: Quite!

Mrs Thompson: It's the police I feel sorry for.

Mrs Fearnley: And they've started with more violence and vandalism.

Mrs Thompson: Blowing up pillar boxes.

Mrs Fearnley: Throwing stones at Lloyd George.

Ethel: That sounds like a good idea.

Lady Amberley: Burning down Kew Gardens Tea Pavilion.

Mrs Fearnley: Beating Mr Asquith with dog-whips.

Ethel: That's an even better idea. I think I'll join them.

Lady Amberley: Putting acid on golf courses.

Wealthy Man: Dammit, is nothing sacred?

Mrs Fearnley: Smashing windows.

Lady Amberley: Fire-raising.

Wealthy Man: What are the police doing about it?

(*A line of Suffragette Suspects enter from stage right, half of them armed with hammers, half with large boxes of matches. A Police Chorus takes up positions behind them.*)

Policemen (*Peering round the suspects, sing*):
Who were you with last night?
Who were you with last night?
It wasn't your sister it wasn't your ma.

Suspects (*Sing*): Ah! Ah! Ah! Ah! – Ah! ah! ah! ah!

Policemen (*Peering round the suspects from opposite side*):
Who were you with last night?
Out in the pale moonlight.
Are you going to tell the police, now you've come home
Who you were with last night?

Suspects (*Stage whisper*): No!

(*General Drummond enters from stage left.*)

General Drummond: Company. 'Shun'.

(*All cast come to attention.*)

General Drummond: Company. Right turn!

(*They do.*)

General Drummond: Answer your names as you go.
Acland, Eleanor.

(*She answers 'Present' and makes a half turn and then goes, as do the others after replying to their names.*)

Ashton, Margaret
Belloc, Elizabeth Rayner
Besant, Annie
Craggs, Helen Millar
Cullen, Louise
Davison, Emily Wilding

(*There is no reply to this one.*)

General Drummond: Where is Emily Wilding Davison?

(*The cast all become a crowd at a race meeting, in the 'stand' at rear of the stage. The crowd cheers on the horses, all in mime. Then there is a scream. All freeze.*)

Narrator (*From the crowd*): Emily Wilding Davison died after throwing herself in front of the King's racehorse Anmer in the Derby of 1913.

Wealthy Man: She couldn't have known it was the King's horse.

Mrs Fearnley: Couldn't she?

Lady Amberley: So now at last they have a real martyr.

Mrs Thompson: I wish I knew who to feel sorry for now.

Wealthy Man: Dammit you never know what these women will get up to next.

Newsboy (*Running in through the auditorium to front centre stage.*): Archduke Ferdinand shot at Sarajevo!

Wealthy Man (*Moving to front of stage*): My God! Now they've gone too far.

Newsgirl (*Running in through auditorium and joining the Newsboy centre stage*): Special! Austria declares war on Serbia!

Newsboy: Russia mobilises! Russia mobilises!

Newsgirl: Government declares truce on Suffragettes!

Newsboy: Suffragettes released from prison!

Newsgirl: Mrs Pankhurst addresses her troops!

(*Mrs Pankhurst moves from the crowd at rear, moves the Wealthy Man out of the way and addresses the audience.*)

Mrs Pankhurst: The militant campaign is over – for the present. A still more powerful enemy has arisen, a more important fight has begun. An opportunity has been given to us to prove our worth alongside the men of this country. There will be no shortage of work for women to do, there will be no work that women will refuse to undertake, and when the end of the conflict finally arrives there will be no doubts in the minds of the country that women deserve the equality of the vote. Work now to earn the vote after the war.

(*As she speaks the cast on stage sing 'It's a long way to Tipperary' – very softly at first, gaining in volume as she does in her speech.*)

Newsgirl: Allies lose 850 000 men in 1914.
Half the British Expeditionary Force wiped out.

Lloyd George (*A Welsh voice from the crowd, rear right*): The women of this country can help, and help enormously. I believe they can help us through to victory. Without them victory will tarry and victory which tarries means victory whose footprints are footprints of blood. We want to shorten the war because it means life, and with life it means curtailing in many cases the burden of sorrow which the war brings.

Newsgirl (1): Ypres: 60 000 men dead.

Newsgirl (2): Aubers Ridge: 12 000 men dead.

Newsgirl (3): Loos: 10 000 men dead.

Newsgirl (1): Somme: 20 000 men dead in one day.

Newsgirl (2): Aisne: 180 000 men dead

Newsgirl (3): Passchendaele: 360 000 casualties

(*In silence the street scene emerges, many dressed in black, with mourning armbands.*)

Lady Bagot: But it was rather fun driving a tractor. What did you do?

Mrs Murray: Munitions . . . and you?

Lady Combermore: I drove an ambulance.

Mrs Fearnley: On the Somme it was, you say?

Mrs Murray: Yes, one of the first casualties he was – it was a shock at the time. I was at the factory when they told me.

Ethel: Working alongside me. You could've knocked me down wiv a feather.

Kathleen: Our Jack's officer he was – didn't last long though . . .

Annie: 'Ow many of them did?

Lady Amberley: Do? Do? Good heavens, my dear, *I* was in America – they're so much more civilised over there, *we* didn't *do* anything!

Mrs Russell: Do you reckon they'll give us the vote now?

Mrs Parkes: I don't see how Asquith can avoid it any longer.

Mrs Thompson: But I wasn't a Suffragette.

Mrs Russell: I still think you should vote.

Mrs Thompson: I never went to prison.

Mrs Parkes: You'll still be allowed to vote.

Mrs Thompson: But I didn't do any war work either.

Mrs Russell: Well?

Mrs Thompson: Well . . . it's *me* that I feel sorry for now.

(*Jeers and cries from the crowd – 'Never mind old luv', 'Serves you right', 'Cheer up, it's all over now'.*)

All (*Sing*):

Pack up your troubles in your old kit-bag,
And smile, smile, smile.
While you've a lucifer to light your fag,
Smile, girls, that's the style.
What's the use of worrying?
It never was worthwhile, so

Pack up your troubles in your old kit-bag
And smile, smile, smile.

(*There could be some impromptu dancing in this chorus.*)

Asquith (*Moving to front centre*):
My opposition to women's suffrage has always been based, and based solely, on considerations of public expediency. I think that some years ago I ventured to use the expression 'let the women work out their own salvation'. Well, they have worked it out during this war. How could we have carried on the war without them? I, therefore, believe – and I believe many others who have hitherto thought with me in this matter – are prepared to acquiesce in the general decision of the majority that some measure of women's suffrage should be conferred.

(*Cheers and shouts of 'Good Old Asquith'.*)

All (*Sing*):
Shout, shout, up with your song!
Cry with the wind, for the dawn is breaking.
March, march, swing you along,
Wide blows our banner and hope is waking.
Song with its story, dreams with their glory,
Lo! they call and glad is their word.
Forward! Hark how it swells,
Thunder of freedom, the voice of the Lord!

Life, strife, these two are one!
Naught can ye win but by faith and daring.
On, on, that ye have done,
But for the work of today preparing.
Firm in reliance, laugh a defiance,
(Laugh in hope, for sure is the end)
March, march, many as one,
Shoulder to shoulder and friend to friend!'

(*The cast line up across stage, two or three ranks deep as they sing this march. CURTAIN on final line.*)

Drama ideas

1 Work in groups of four or five. Imagine that you are the members of an Edwardian family, with a very domineering father, whose word is law. One of you is the sixteen-year old daughter of the family. Some Suffragette pamphlets have been found in the daughter's bedroom, perhaps by a servant or an older sister. How will the family react? Will anyone be brave enough to side with the daughter, and sympathise with her views?

2 Work with a partner. One of you, A, is a young girl who wants to get a worthwhile job. The other, B, is an older person whom A trusts and confides in. What advice will B give A about career opportunities?

Try two versions of the scene; in one, A is from a wealthy background, in the other she is from a very poor family. Change roles, and repeat the interview, but this time it is the 1980s and B is a Careers Adviser.

3 Devise a series of tableaux or 'still pictures' showing what might have been regarded as the 'ideal' life of a woman at the beginning of the century – before the Suffragette campaign.

Then change the scenes to show the ways in which you think life has changed for women in the 1980s.

4 In groups of three or four work out some humorous scenes involving Suffragettes chaining themselves to railings. These could be completely in mime or might include speech. Perhaps you could improvise a scene in which a policeman is distracted in some way by a Suffragette while a second Suffragette fastens herself to the railings. When the policeman realises he has been tricked and tries to release the chained Suffragette, the other one chains herself to the same railings. Or perhaps in attempting to release the Suffragettes the policeman might himself end up being chained. Try the scene out in slow motion or even double speed, like film run at the wrong speed, for the maximum humorous effect.

5 Work with a partner. Imagine that one of you is an old lady who was once part of the Suffragette campaign. The other is a young friend or relative. How will the old lady remember her experiences? Was the struggle for votes worthwhile?

Follow-up work

1 Work with a partner. Imagine that you are two Suffragettes imprisoned in nearby cells in Strangeways Prison, Manchester. One of you is Edith, the daughter of a wealthy family. The other, Molly, is a poor working-class girl.

During exercise one day you find a moment to talk to each other without being overheard by the wardresses. Take it in turn to tell each other what you find hardest to bear about being in prison. What do you each miss most from your life at home?

Each of you write a short letter home. What will be the most important things to include in your letter?

2 Queen Victoria disapproved of women who wanted the vote, and thought they deserved to be whipped. Write a short scene, serious or humorous, showing what might have taken place if the Queen had met Mrs Pankhurst.

3 Work in a group of three. One of you supports the Suffragettes, the second opposes their ideas. If you like, you can choose to be one of the characters in the play. The third member of the group is a reporter, sent to interview the others. After the interview, work together to write up the newspaper article, including an eye-catching headline.

4 Write and make a pamphlet about 'Votes for Women', that might have been handed out at a meeting in 1905. Make your pamphlet look eighty years old, not just in the writing but in the condition of the paper. Imagine that the pamphlet is to be exhibited in a museum, and make an explanatory card to be exhibited alongside the document.

For discussion

1 There are now considerably more careers open to women than used to be the case. Do you think men and women are equally capable in every job? Are there any jobs that you feel (although men and women *can* do them) are done better, or more satisfactorily, by one sex?

2 In the 1890s the role of the woman in society was assisted in its change by, amazingly, the new game of lawn tennis, and the development of the bicycle. Lawn tennis required greater freedom of dress in order for it to be played well, and bicycling was an interest which could not easily be chaperoned – giving girls the opportunity to make unexpected

acquaintances. Today, freedom of dressing and meeting whom you wish is almost taken for granted. Do you think it necessary in any way to impose limitations on how young people dress or whom they associate with? Are there any situations today that exist where you think it necessary to dress in a specific way in order to conform?

3 One argument that was used again and again against granting women the vote was that, if married, they would vote as their husband voted or, if unmarried, as their father voted. How true do you think this might have been at the turn of the century, and how true would you consider it is today?

4 To judge from the turn-out of voters at local and national elections, many people who are eligible to vote do not actually do so. How might people be encouraged to vote in important elections? If people do not bother to vote, should they have the right to vote taken away from them?

Reference Books

Roger Fulford, *Votes for Women*, Faber and Faber
Trevor Lloyd, *Suffragettes International*, Library of the 20th Century
Midge Mackenzie, *Shoulder to Shoulder*, Penguin

Sources for music

'Fall in and Follow Me' by Mills & Bennett (Feldman)
'I Was a Good Little Girl 'til I Met You' by Harris & Tate (Francis, Day & Hunter)
'Oh Dear What Can the Matter Be?' Trad.
'Father, Hear the Prayer we Offer' (Hymn)
'Put Me Amongst the Girls' by Murphy & Lipton (Feldman)
'Who were you with Last Night' by Godrey & Sheridan (Feldman)
'It's a Long Way to Tipperary' by Jack Judge & Harry Williams (Feldman)
'Pack Up Your Troubles' by Asaf & Powell (Francis, Day & Hunter)
'The March of the Women' by Ethel Smyth (Breitkopf & Härtel)

Titanic

The 'Titanic' *goes down: a painter's impression*

Introduction

To cross the Atlantic in style today we might well book a flight on Concorde. It is fast, it is comfortable, and it has prestige. At the turn of the century the equivalent would have been a large, expensive, luxurious liner; considerably slower, but with all possible comforts, elegance, and prestige.

At that time the various steamship companies of Europe and North America competed with each other to provide the very best in terms of both luxury and speed, and the ship that held the 'Blue Riband' for the fastest Atlantic crossing brought acclaim and prestige not only to its company, but also to its country of origin. In 1897 Germany had gained the Blue Riband with the liner *Wilhelm der Grosse*, only to see it pass in 1900 to another German vessel, the *Deutschland* when it made the crossing in five days, seven hours and thirty-eight minutes. This record remained in German hands until 1907, when a Cunard liner, the *Lusitania*, achieved a crossing in five days and fifty-four minutes, bringing the record to England. The Cunard Steamship Company's chief rival in England was The White Star Line, and the *Lusitania*'s success prompted White Star to plan a worthy liner for their fleet which might itself take the coveted Blue Riband. In fact the company had two liners built, first the *Olympic* and then the *Titanic*. The *Titanic* was thought to be the ultimate in size, luxury and, it was hoped, speed. What is more it was considered to be unsinkable.

No expense had been spared in the fitting-out of the ship's interior. Apart from the more usual accommodation there was a gymnasium, a turkish bath, a squash court, a swimming pool, hair-dressers, elegant verandas, the Café Parisien with artificial sunlight, and a most imposing collection of suites for really wealthy passengers. Only one feature had in any way been skimped on the ship, and that was the provision of lifeboats. While there was accommodation for 2300 people, there were only enough lifeboats for 1200. The regulations set down by the Board of Trade made it unnecessary to provide more, but then when such regulations had been drawn up no one had envisaged a liner of such a tremendous size.

On Wednesday, 10 April 1912, the *Titanic* sailed from Southampton on its maiden Atlantic crossing. On board were 1300 passengers and almost 900 crew. The passengers were sailing either First Class, Second Class or Third Class and the accommodation clearly showed the class-divisions among the passengers. There were many very well-known and prosperous individuals travelling First Class, including Colonel J. J. Astor and his wife; Mr Ben Guggenheim; and Mr Harry Widener – all millionaires; Mr and Mrs Isador Straus – founders of the famous Macy's Store in Philadelphia, and Mr William T. Stead, a leading British reformer and newspaper editor. The Second Class, the smallest of the passenger groups, was a cross-section of what we might call the middle-class – shopkeepers, schoolteachers, clergymen, engineers – many returning from European visits, some beginning a visit to relations in America. The Third Class contingent included many people from Ireland, and was comprised mainly of those seeking their fortunes in the New World. The passenger list was a cross-section of society from the extremely rich to the very poor. There were also on board 3418 sacks of mail, five grand pianos, and a number of precious items including a rare copy of the book *The Rubaiyat of Omar Khayyam*, bound in gold and inlaid with precious stones.

The *Titanic* called at Cherbourg and Queenstown (now Cork) to pick up more passengers, then set course for the Atlantic. Icebergs were always a hazard in the North Atlantic at this time of the year. The Arctic pack-ice breaks up and drifts south, and in 1912 it happened earlier than usual. Captain Smith on the *Titanic* received several warnings of large icebergs from ships already in the Atlantic, but possibly driven by a desire to achieve a Blue Riband crossing on the ship's maiden voyage, he chose to ignore them. No reduction in speed was ordered, no extra look-outs were posted, and those that were on duty were not equipped with binoculars.

At twenty minutes to midnight on Sunday 14 April, the *Titanic* collided with a large iceberg. The passengers and crew felt only the slightest judder, but the collision had left a gash some 100 metres far below the ship's waterline. Water rushed into the ship's first five so-called 'watertight' compartments, and as they filled up and the bow of the ship tilted forward, so the water flowed over these compartments' divisions into each succeeding section. Gradually the ship tipped further and further forward, and at twenty minutes past two on Monday morning, 15 April, only two hours and forty minutes after the collision, the *Titanic* slid below the calm surface of an icy sea.

The radio operator had sent distress messages using, for the very first time, the new call-sign 'S.O.S.' Fifty-eight miles away, the Cunard ship *Carpathia* raced to the rescue. The *Californian*, only ten miles away, ignored the *Titanic* – their radio operator was off duty and the crew asleep. On board the *Titanic* the ship's orchestra played to the very end. 'Women and children first' had been the cry, but it had also been 'First Class first, then Second Class and then. . . .'

Of the 322 First Class passengers, 202 were saved.
Of the 277 Second Class passengers, 115 were saved.
Of the 709 Third Class passengers, 176 were saved.
Of the 898 crew members, 210 were saved.

The loss of the Titanic remains the biggest civilian sea disaster.

Staging the play

The presentation of this documentary on stage demands a 'music-hall' style, rather like that of the original *Oh What a Lovely War*. Several characters act very much as a narrator or Master of Ceremonies, others are obvious comedians or 'straight men'. Between them they outline the action and set the various scenes. You should aim to present the characters almost as caricatures, representing 'types' rather than subtle individuals. This should extend even to the named characters who should also be presented larger than life: e.g. Captain Smith as the English gentleman; Bruce Ismay as a somewhat unscrupulous, conceited, upper-class businessman; Fleet, the look-out, as the cockney seaman, and so on.

Since characters appear only briefly, they can be portrayed adequately by either boys or girls. All cast will need to contribute in the songs, though no great talent for singing is needed. Try to keep the costuming simple. Each member of cast could wear the same basic outfit of, say, jeans and a white shirt or blouse, to which items can be added to suggest the part they are playing at a particular time. Pirie and Ismay could use top-hats, Captain Smith, a peaked cap; the Teacher, a gown; the Dockers, caps and waistcoats; upper-class ladies, a long skirt; steerage passengers, shawls; and so on. You will need to ensure well-rehearsed use of these changes, particularly if you have one member of cast playing several roles.

The character who speaks the verses from the *Rubaiyat* perhaps needs singling out a little more obviously – maybe in a different colour, for this character represents the spirit of the poem and the lines have a particular aptness to the events of the play.

In production, the director needs to keep a good pace, making the performance slick and crisp. The humorous intention of many of the scenes should contrast strongly with the harsh facts of the tragedy. In the actual staging of the piece you could experiment with the use of levels, and properties that can perhaps have a double or treble use – rostra can create individual lifeboat areas, or be tables and chairs, the bridge and the crow's nest. You should find also that it helps groupings on stage if more levels are available. It may well help the staging if a large drawing of the *Titanic* can be introduced into the planning scenes of the play: you might even make use of projected images for these scenes and for other settings throughout the play. In the first production of this documentary the *Titanic* was drawn on a run of seven short stage flats, which were reversed to suggest other scenes – all was done as part of the action, and the flats hand-held by the cast themselves. Don't be afraid of using the auditorium – for exits and entrances and for 'pointing' certain scenes, such as the positions of other vessels at the time of the sinking; and the edge of the stage can be used as a feature in rescuing survivors from the sea. Although it was planned for a proscenium stage, the play would lose nothing by a thrust stage or even in-the-round presentation.

There are few sound effects in the play, and it should be possible to obtain the necessary ship's bell, or similar, and a teacher's whistle. The sound of 'ripping' that represents the collision with the iceberg, can be made by tearing a stiff piece of canvas or heavy sheeting – but this will need some experimenting with, to achieve the most effective sound. The radio sounds can be made also by the cast or by an electronic keyboard or something similar.

There is no real need for elaborate lighting, though some directors may like to have it. It does add considerably, however, to the impact of the play if the lights can dim to darkness during the singing of 'Nearer my God to Thee', and then be brought up again gradually.

Titanic

The characters

Singer (this part could be shared)
Comedian
M.C.
Narrator
'1898'
'1907'
Mr Mansfield, a publisher
Morgan Robertson, an author
Bruce Ismay, director of the White Star Line
Lord Pirie, chairman of Harland and Wolff, Shipbuilders
Teacher
Pat, **Paddy**, **Mike**, **Jimmy** } Irish dockers
Spirit
Captain of the *Titanic* (Captain Smith)
Higginbottom, a self-made millionaire
Steward
Fleet, **Mate** } Lookouts
Mr Murdoch, First Officer on the *Titanic*
Sailors 1–10
S.S. *CARPATHIA*
S.S. *CALIFORNIA*
Radio Operator
Fanshawe, **Carruthers**, **Maltravers** } upper-class young men

The first performance by the Dewsbury Arts Group (Youth section)

Digby	upper-class young men
Cuthbert	
Pickering	
Jenkins, a seaman	
Lucinda	upper-class ladies
Gertrude	
Mabel	
Agatha	
Dora	
Purser	
Stoker	Boat One
Woman	
Officer	Boat Two
Mr Straus	
Mrs Straus	
Lady	Boat Three
Man	
Maid	
Gentleman	Boat Four
'Foreigner'	
Girl	
Countess	Boat Five
Woman 2	
Lady	Boat Six
Officer	
Man	

Auditorium lights fade down slowly: an introduction to 'Rule, Britannia' is played and the curtain opens. On stage the entire cast (except the M.C.) stand around, the Singer standing on a platform carrying a large Union Jack. He or she sings . . .

Singer: When Britain first at Heaven's command,
Arose from out the azure main,
Arose from out, arose from out the azure main,
This was the charter, the charter of the land,
And guardian angels sang this strain.

(*All cast turn to face the audience, very formally.*)

All: Rule Britannia! Britannia rules the waves;
Britons never, never, never shall be . . .

(*One character detaches himself/herself from the group and steps forward stage left and sings. . .*)

Comedian: . . . mar-ri-ed to a mer-ma-id
At the bottom of the deep blue sea.

(*The rest of the cast relax their positions and re-group into more informal poses.*)

Comedian (*Moving to front centre position*):
Oh 'twas in the broad Atlantic,
'Mid the equinoctial gales,
That a young fellow fell overboard
Among the sharks and whales
And down he went like a streak of light,
So quickly down went he,
Until he came to a mer-ma-id,
At the bottom of the deep blue sea.

All: Singing Rule Britannia, Britannia rules the waves!
Britons never, never, never, shall be
. . . mar-ri-ed to a mer-ma-id
At the bottom of the deep blue sea.

(*Singer joins Comedian centre stage.*)

Singer: We sent a boat to look for him,
Expecting to find his corpse,
When up he came with a bang and a shout,
And a voice sepulchrally hoarse,
My comrades and my messmates,
O do not look for me,
For I'm mar-ri-ed to a mer-ma-id
At the bottom of the deep blue sea.

All: Singing Rule Britannia, Britannia rules the waves!
Britons never, never, never shall be
. . . mar-ri-ed to a mer-ma-id
At the bottom of the deep blue sea!

(*The cast applaud and congratulate themselves. Enter M.C. from stage left.*)

M.C.: Right, off you go then! That's enough of that!

(*The cast exit right and left, chatting to each other about the success of the first number.*)

M.C.: Now then . . . good evening, Ladies and Gentlemen, – tonight I'd like to present to you a little monologue – a little monologue entitled – 'The Wreck of the Hesperus'.

(*Comedian enters stage right, now perhaps wearing a clown outfit, or a striped blazer and red nose, or similar; he proffers a note to the M.C.*)

M.C.: Go away, not now, can't you see I'm busy . . . it's a little recitation entitled . . .

(*Comedian nudges him.*)

Oh no! Not again. Do you mind . . . ladies and gentlemen . . . a little recitation entitled . . .

(*Comedian nudges him more firmly and proffers the note.*)

. . . All right! All right! You win . . . (*Takes note. The Comedian retires to stage right.*) Ladies and Gentlemen, before I make my dramatic recitation I have a small announcement to make: . . . 'Do you believe in E.S.P.?'

Comedian: Does it wash whiter?

M.C.: Don't be silly! I'm reading what it says here . . . 'Do you believe in E.S.P. – Extra-sensory Perception?'

Comedian (*Joining the M.C. at centre*): Extra-sensory what?

M.C.: Perception.

Comedian: Rubbish!

M.C.: It means being able to predict what is going to happen in the future.

Comedian: Predict?

M.C.: To somehow gain insight about events that are yet to happen – often years ahead!

Comedian: What a lot of old . . . I mean what an amazing load of . . . (*Directly to the audience*) Do you believe it? What a . . .

M.C.: Knowing in advance, by some spiritual method, about events yet to come . . .

Comedian: Impossible!

M.C. (*Referring to the note*): Ladies and Gentlemen, there will be a meeting here next week to discuss the evidence of the existence of Extra-sensory Perception.

(*M.C. exits stage left.*)

Comedian: You know . . . I knew he was going to say that.

(*Comedian exits stage right, as a Narrator appears from the rear left of the stage and walks forward.*)

Narrator: In 1898 a struggling author named Morgan Robertson wrote a novel . . . (*Robertson enters stage right with a novel in manuscript form.*) . . . about a fabulous

Atlantic liner, far larger than any that had ever been built. Robertson loaded his ship with rich and complacent people and then wrecked it one cold April night on an iceberg. This somehow showed the futility of the whole undertaking, and in fact the book was entitled *Futility* when it appeared that year published by the firm of M. F. Mansfield.

(*Narrator exits stage left: two banner-carriers enter stage left and stage right and take up a position: the banners read '1898' and '1907'.*)

'1898' (*Stage right.*) The scene: the publishing office of the firm M. F. Mansfield.

'1907' (*Stage left.*) The scene: Devonshire House, the home of Lord Pirie, Chairman of Harland and Wolff, Shipbuilders of Belfast.

(*Enter Mansfield from stage right to Robertson.*)

Mansfield (*Taking manuscript*): I'll be absolutely honest with you, Robertson, I have read your manuscript and find it more than a little far-fetched.

Robertson: Far-fetched, Mr Mansfield?

Mansfield: Tea-from-china, Robertson. Ludicrous, if you prefer it.

Robertson: Imaginative, surely, Mr Mansfield?

Mansfield: What? Oh yes – I grant you that, Robertson. You do have imagination.

(*Mansfield and Robertson look through the manuscript. Ismay and Pirie enter stage left, each with a glass.*)

Ismay: We are men with imagination are we not, Lord Pirie?

Pirie: I would like to think so, Mr Ismay . . . a little more claret?

Ismay: And in my position as Director of the White Star Line, I need to be looking to the future. . . . Thank you!

(*'1907' tops up Ismay's glass.*)

Pirie: So what are you suggesting?

Ismay: At least two new liners . . . built to be the largest and most luxurious afloat.

Pirie: By Harland and Wolff, I trust?

Ismay: Of course . . . who else?

(*They laugh and drink.*)

Mansfield: I know the public are used to the writings of Mr Jules Verne – but he is a Frenchman, you know – *our* reading public is, I believe, more educated and less gullible, less easily led by fantasy and fairy stories.

Robertson: This is no fairy story, Mr Mansfield.

Mansfield: I can't see it, Robertson!

(*They peruse the manuscript again.*)

Pirie: What do you envisage?

Ismay: The ultimate in luxury, in space, in elegance . . .

Pirie: . . . and speed . . . don't forget speed, Ismay.

Ismay: . . . and speed . . . of course . . . speed . . .

Pirie: Is it a feasible project?

Ismay: Let's map out some ideas. Look here.

(*He 'draws' the* Titanic *on a wall, or the back of the 1907 banner, or it is brought on, or projected – ideally the audience should be able to see an image of the ship from here on.*

The two groups now continue their conversations, together, and ultimately they overlap – this will need careful balancing of voices and good timing.)

Mansfield: You write about a new liner – a luxury liner?

Robertson: Correct. 800 feet long.

Pirie: This would mean we're looking to a vessel at least 800 feet long.

Ismay: Slightly more, I think.

Mansfield: Displacement 70 000 tons.

Robertson: That's right.

Pirie: And a displacement of what . . . 66 000 tons?

Ismay: Say 70 000 tons to be on the safe side.

Mansfield: Triple screw?

Pirie: Triple screw!

Robertson: Making 24/25 knots.

Ismay: Capable of 24/25 knots.

Mansfield
Pirie
Robertson
Ismay } (*Out to audience*): The biggest in the world!!

Mansfield: You then ask us to believe that this liner, full of rich passengers, is lost on its maiden voyage through collision with an iceberg.

Robertson: A possibility.

Mansfield: Sensationalism of the most tasteless kind . . .

Robertson: But Mr Mansfield . . .

Ismay: Spacious dining saloon.

Pirie: Smoking rooms.

Ismay: Gymnasia.

Pirie: Turkish baths.

Ismay: Lifts.

Pirie: Covered promenades.

Ismay: Electric heaters.

Pirie: Bedsteads four feet wide.

Mansfield: You then imply that because of its size, speed and construction the vessel was considered unsinkable – and that this confidence led to the vessel not being equipped with an adequate complement of lifeboats and life-saving equipment for the passengers and crew.

Ismay: At least!

Pirie: Mahogany.

Ismay: Palm trees.

Pirie: Cut glass.

Ismay: Chandeliers.

Pirie: Oysters.

Ismay: Grand pianos.

Pirie: Axminsters.

Ismay: Roast duckling.

Pirie: Pâté de foie gras.

Ismay: Waldorf pudding.

Pirie: Peaches in chartreuse jelly.

(*Each of these two sections gains in momentum with the enthusiasm of the characters, but ends at the same time – then there is a brief pause.*)

Pirie: What about lifeboats?

Ismay: For what?. . . . It'll be unsinkable.

Pirie: We'll do it!

Mansfield: We'll print it!

Ismay: We will!

Robertson: We will?

Mansfield: What's your liner called?

Ismay: And we'll call them . . .

Pirie: The *Olympic* and . . .

Robertson: The *Titan*, Mr Mansfield.

(*Banner-carrier '1898', Mansfield and Robertson exit stage right.*)

Ismay: . . . and . . . and the . . .

Pirie: . . . the . . . er . . . um . . . the . . . um . . .

(*Comedian enters from stage left and comes to centre, talking to the audience.*)

Comedian: What do *you* think they called it?

(*If the audience replies* 'Titanic':)

Very good, sir (or madam). You've won yourself a lifejacket – you may need it later on!

(OR, *if no audience reply is forthcoming*:)

Ismay:
Pirie: } The *Titanic*!

Comedian: Well done, lads – go get yourselves lifejackets – you'll need them later on!

(*Sings*)
Oh they built the ship *Titanic* to sail the ocean blue
And they thought they had a ship that the water would never go through,
But the Lord's almighty hand
Knew that ship would never land.
It was sad when that great ship went down.

(*The bulk of the cast re-enter, dressed as characters of the time, and group to act as chorus as they all sing.*)

All (*Entering*):
It was sad (it was sad),
It was sad (mighty sad),
It was sad when that great ship went down.
Husbands and wives, little children lost their lives.
It was sad when that great ship went down.

Singer (*Taking up a prominent position*): I name this ship *Titanic*, may God bless her and all who sail in her!

(*The crowd cheers, hats are thrown in the air, etc. and the* Titanic *chorus repeated. Some groups may perform an impromptu dance.*)

All (*Enthusiastically*):
It was sad (it was sad),
It was sad (mighty sad),
It was sad when that great ship went down.
Husbands and wives, little children lost their lives.
It was sad when that great ship went down.

(*Comedian and the M.C. come forward centre.*)

Comedian: I say, I say, I say – what do you get if you cross the Atlantic with the *Titanic*?

M.C.: I don't know, what *do* you get if you cross the Atlantic with the *Titanic*?

Comedian: Half-way!

(*Laughter, or groans, from the cast on stage. Teacher enters from stage left.*)

Teacher: All right! All right! Quiet now! Settle down there . . . (*The cast on stage, sit as is convenient on the rostra or levels or floor*) – and sit up straight (*and speaking to the audience*) – and I mean all of you! Pay attention. Now the *Titanic* was in fact about eleven storeys high – stop chewing at the back there – and a sixth of a mile long. Perhaps her most interesting feature – and don't talk while I'm talking – was her completely watertight construction. she had a double bottom – and I don't expect laughter from you – and was divided into sixteen watertight compartments. These were formed by fifteen watertight bulkheads (*Spells it.*) B-U-L-K-H-E-A-D-S – which are walls or divisions each running across the width of the ship

– do stop doing that at the back . . . The *Titanic* could float with any two compartments completely flooded – it could float with. . . . What *are* you doing at the back there? . . . I won't warn you again – what are you playing about with?

(*Teacher exits through the audience: the cast on stage become Irish dockers loading cargo. Comedian and M.C. exit stage right. Movement involving the passing of cargo should be mimed.*)

Pat: Come on, you lot, move that luggage and cargo along. We don't want to miss the tide, do we?

Paddy: I'll be glad to see the back-end of all this.

Mike: You're right there.

Paddy: I've never seen such cargo and luggage.

Mike: You're not wrong.

Paddy: Look at this – sixteen trunks for Mr & Mrs Ryerson.

Mike: That's a lot.

Paddy: Sixteen trunks? For one family. That's more than a lot.

Mike: Unless they're elephants.

Paddy: What?

Mike: A family of elephants.

Paddy: And what do you mean by that?

Jimmy: Eight hundred cases of shelled walnuts!

Mike: Eight hundred cases of shelled walnuts!

Paddy: That should come in 'andy.

Jimmy: Thirty cases of golf clubs and tennis rackets for Mr Spalding.

Mike: Eight dozen tennis balls for R. F. Downey and Company.

Jimmy: Thirty thousand fresh eggs.

Paddy: Thirty thousand fresh eggs.

Mike: Thirty thousand fresh eggs.

Pat: Thirty thousand fresh eggs.

Jimmy: Five Grand Pianos.

Paddy: Five Grand Pianos.

Mike: Five Grand Pianos.

Pat: Five Grand Pianos.

Jimmy: Fifteen thousand bottles of ale and stout.

Paddy: Fifteen thousand bottles of ale and . . . Guinness.

Mike: That's more like it.

Jimmy: One jewelled copy of *The Rubaiyat of Omar Khayyam*.

Paddy: One jewelled Ruby Yat belonging to some foreign bloke.

Mike: A what?

Paddy: A Ruby Yat!

Mike: What's that then?

Pat: Look it's all written down. One copy of *The Rubaiyat of Omar Khayyam*.

Mike: Poetry is it?

Pat: Priceless.

Mike: 'Ere that reminds me. Did you 'ear the one about . . .

(*The Dockers cluster round Mike to hear his joke: they freeze and the Spirit character enters from stage left*.)

Spirit: 'Awake! for morning in the Bowl of Night
Has flung the Stone that puts the Stars to Flight:

And lo! The Hunter of the East has caught
The Sultan's Turret in a Noose of Light!'

(*Spirit exits stage right. Singer enters stage left and moves to centre.*)

Singer (*Sings*):
So they loaded all the cargo
And the luggage down below
The passengers all came aboard, the tugs began to tow,
The first-class rich, third-class poor
Two thousand souls, two hundred more.
It was sad when that great ship went down.

(*Narrator enters stage right and stands stage right: the words are spoken over the chorus, sung quietly by all on stage. The Dockers break their 'freeze' and group in relaxed positions.*)

Narrator: On April 10, 1912, the *Titanic* left Southampton on her maiden voyage to New York. Her cargo and passenger list was collectively worth 250 million dollars. On her way over she struck an iceberg.

All: It was sad (it was sad)
It was sad (mighty sad)
It was sad when that great ship went down
Husbands and wives, little children lost their lives,
It was sad when that great ship went down.

(*Comedian enters stage right, M.C. enters stage left, they meet centre.*)

Comedian: I say, I say, I say, do you want any jobs doing at home?

M.C.: Jobs?

Comedian: Around the house – plumbing or joinery.

M.C.: Not by you, you're an amateur – give me a professional any time.

Comedian: The *Titanic* was built by professionals. Noah was an amateur.

(*Ship's bell rings.*)

Narrator: Three cheers for the *Titanic*! Hip-hip . . .

(*The cast reply with three cheers then 'freeze'. The Spirit character enters stage left and stands stage left.*)

Spirit: 'The Wordly Hope men set their Hearts upon
Turns Ashes – or it prospers; and anon,
Like Snow upon the Desert's dusty Face
Lighting a little Hour or two – is gone.'

(*Break the 'freeze': the scene is now the bridge of the* Titanic. *The cast move offstage to leave only enough to represent crew: perhaps a ship's wheel could be brought on. Ismay enters with Captain Smith from stage left.*)

Ismay: Captain Smith.

Captain: Mr Ismay?

Ismay: And how is she handling?

Captain: Well – thank you.

Ismay: She's to your liking, then?

Captain: I have no complaints at all.

Ismay: And her speed, Captain?

Captain: More than adequate.

Ismay: Could we be moving faster still, then?

Captain: We are not at full speed, Mr Ismay; the route we travel is, as you are well aware, the Northern Atlantic Route. At this time of year ice is a considerable hazard at these latitudes. My first consideration must be for the passengers.

Ismay: But what of the Company, Captain? If we could

produce a fast crossing, the Line would become the foremost in Atlantic crossings. We would have a secure future.

Captain: Secure?

Ismay: We are in a very competitive business, Captain. Our livelihoods, *all* our livelihoods, depend on our keeping the name of the Line in the public eye.

Captain: Even if it involves danger?

Ismay: Captain, this vessel is unsinkable, it is the ultimate in design and construction. (*Pause.*) Full speed ahead?

Captain: If you insist.

(*Spirit enters and stands stage right.*)

Spirit: 'Ah, make the most of what we yet may spend,
Before we too into the Dust descend;
Dust into Dust, and under Dust, to lie,
Sans Wine, sans Song, sans Singer, and sans End!'

(*Ship's bell rings. Spirit exits stage right.*
Scene change: the dining saloon. The bridge scene and characters can remain at the rear of stage and this scene be played in front. Higginbottom enters stage left, Steward from stage right.)

Higginbottom: Ah! There you are, steward!

Steward: Yes, sir?

Higginbottom: I've been looking for you – do you know who I am?

Steward: Sir?

Higginbottom: Well, I'll tell you lad – I'm Arnold 'igginbottom – self-made millionaire – made me money out of pigs, don't cher know – everything but the squeak. First journey abroad this is – everything of the very best –

stateroom – first class – all paid for cash on the nail – you understand?

Steward: Yes sir – of course, sir!

Higginbottom: So what's this, then? (*He produces a card.*)

Steward: It's an invitation to dine at the Captain's table, sir.

Higginbottom: It's a what? What cheek! Not me! Not likely! Do you think after I've spent all this money that I'm going to eat with the crew?

(*He exits stage right, the Steward follows. Comedian makes a quick entrance from stage left to centre.*)

Comedian (*Sings*):

Biggest boat, yet afloat
Full of rich and plenty
Makes a splash – cuts a dash –
Looks unsinkable, it's quite unthinkable.
What a size, big surprise –
Built for the Atlantic
T-I-T-A-N-I-C – *Titanic*! *Titanic*!'

(*All the cast on stage sing a reprise of this chorus as fast as possible Even a tap-dance could be introduced! At end of song all the cast exit. Narrator enters from stage right.*)

Narrator: Sunday, 14 April 1912 – 11.40 p.m. at the masthead.

(*The masthead is a high level at the rear of the stage. Narrator exits stage right. Sound of wind.*)

Fleet: Blow this for a game of soldiers!

Mate: You can say that again.

Fleet: It's cold enough up here to freeze the motto off a Christmas card.

Mate: You can say that again.

Fleet: Look out for icebergs, they say.

Mate: That's right.

Fleet: Never seen it so smooth.

Mate: Like a baby's bottle.!

Fleet: Blimey, look there!

Mate: Where?

Fleet: Dead ahead – see the size of it!

(*The Mate whistles.*
Ship's bell rings. Mr Murdoch enters front stage left.)

Murdoch: Bridge here.

Fleet: Fleet here, sir – masthead lookout.

Murdoch: What did you see?

Fleet: Iceberg dead ahead, sir.

Murdoch: Thank you.

Fleet: Now all you've got to do is move the bloody ship. I reckon you've got about 35 seconds.

(*The cast enter, except Captain and Teacher and begin counting quietly 1 to 35. Comedian enters stage right to centre and talks to audience.*)

Comedian: There was this magician travelling on a luxury liner – entertaining the guests, you see. And the captain, he had a pet parrot that went everywhere with him – a really good talker it was, too. Well, every time the magician did a trick – you know every time he'd make something disappear, the parrot would call out 'It's up his sleeve' or 'It's in his pocket!' . . . and spoiled every trick. The magician was furious. Then, one night during his conjuring act the ship hit an iceberg and sank. The following morning all that could be seen was a piece of driftwood floating about with the magician on one end and the parrot on the other. A few minutes passed and then the parrot said 'All right, wise guy, you win – where've you put the bloody ship?'.

All: Thirty five.

(*Followed by a long ripping noise.*

Obviously the telling of the joke and the counting must be timed to ensure the accuracy required.

Captain enters stage left to Murdoch.)

Captain: Mr Murdoch, what was that?

Murdoch: An iceberg, sir. I put her hard-a-starboard and reversed the engines, and I was going hard-a-port around it, but she was too close. I couldn't do any more, sir.

Captain: Close the emergency doors.

Murdoch: The doors are already closed, sir.

Captain: Obtain a damage report.

Murdoch: Very good, sir.

(*This next section of speeches increases in pace and volume.*)

Sailor 1: Water in the forepeak, sir.

Sailor 2: Water in No. 1 Hold, sir.

Sailor 3: Water in No. 2 Hold, sir.

Sailor 4: Water in mail room, sir.

Sailor 5: . . . in Boiler Room No. 6, sir.

Sailor 6: . . . . . . Boiler Room No. 5, 14 feet above keel level.

Sailor 7: She's making water fast.

Sailor 8: Shut the dampers.

Sailor 9: Draw the fires.

Sailor 10: Get all the pumps going.

Murdoch: Reports indicate a 300-foot gash with the first five compartments hopelessly flooded.

Captain (*Calmly*): Thank you, Mr Murdoch.

(*The cast on stage 'freeze' and the Teacher re-enters through the audience, speaking as he/she does so.*)

Teacher: Now what does this mean? If you'd been watching and listening you'd know the answer. Hands up! Don't shout out. What does all this mean? Yes . . . it would mean that you'd need to wear your wellingtons, Stephen . . . but what else? Your mackintosh. . . . Well, let me tell you. You see the *Titanic* could float with any two of her sixteen watertight compartments flooded. She could float with any three of her first five compartments flooded. She could even float with all of her first four compartments gone. But she could not float with all of her first five compartments full. Now since the division between the fifth and sixth compartments did not go the full height of the hull – if the first five compartments were flooded, the bow would sink so low that the water in the fifth would overflow into the sixth, and then the seventh and then . . .

(*Teacher exits stage right. 'Freeze' breaks.*)

Murdoch: Do you think the ship is seriously damaged, sir?

Captain: I'm afraid she is, Mr Murdoch – I'm afraid she is . . . (*Sings*)
I'll stick to the ship, lads,
You save your lives
I've no one to love me
You've children and wives.
You take to the boats, lads,
Praying to heaven above,
But I'll go down in the angry deep,
With the ship I love.

Send the call for assistance. (*He exits stage left.*)

(*Narrator enters stage right and stands.*)

Narrator: The clock in the wireless cabin said 12.45 a.m. when the *Titanic* sent the first S.O.S. ever sent by an ocean liner.

(*The morse S.O.S. is heard. Teacher re-enters from stage right to centre.*)

Teacher: Right then – positions, please, for the sinking. The *Titanic* over here. (*A group moves to stage right and stands in close order.*) Come on, move along, and start listing a bit. Now then. The other ships – the *Carpathia* was 58 miles away. You go and be the *Carpathia* . . . (*One member of cast moves off into the auditorium.*) – no, further back.

Carpathia: Here?

Teacher: Further back.

Carpathia: Here?

Teacher: That'll do. Ten miles away was the *Californian*. That's you – over there. (*Sends the* Californian *to stage left. The* Californian *leans against the proscenium arch.*) And stand up straight! Now send the messages.

Radio operator: MGY *Titanic*. S.O.S. MGY *Titanic*, S.O.S. Position 41.46 N. 50.14 W.

Teacher: Did you hear that, *Carpathia*?

Carpathia: Coming as fast as we can. Estimate about four hours.

Radio operator: MGY *Titanic*. S.O.S. MGY *Titanic*, S.O.S. Position 41.46 N. 50.14 W.

Teacher: And on the *Californian* . . .

(*But the* Californian *is asleep and snoring.*)

Singer (*At rear, sings*):
Oh they put the lifeboats out
O'er the raging stormy sea,
And the band on board played 'Nearer my God to Thee'.
Little children wept and cried
As the waves swept o'er the side.
It was sad when that great ship went down.

All: It was sad (it was sad),
It was sad (mighty sad),
It was sad when that great ship went down.
Husbands and wives, little children lost their lives.
It was sad when that great ship went down.

(*All cast now take up positions to represent different lifeboat groups as the chorus finishes. Teacher exits stage right. Captain enters stage left.*)

Captain: Abandon ship! Women and children first! (*Exits through audience.*)

(*Panic! Ad-libbed conversations, directions and arguments. A whistle is blown: cast 'freeze'.*)

Singer (*Sings*):
And as the humble closed their eyes
In the darkness of the hold,
The rich upstairs were playing cards for gold,
And they laughed when a sailor said,
'There's an iceberg close ahead'.
It was sad when that great ship went down.

All (*Sing, subdued*):
It was sad (it was sad),
It was sad (mighty sad),
It was sad when that great ship went down.
Husbands and wives, little children lost their lives,
It was sad when that great ship went down.

(*During the chorus an upper-class group is formed, playing

bridge at stage right: another group becomes the steerage passengers at stage left.)

Fanshawe: A heart.

Carruthers: No bid.

Maltravers: Two clubs.

Digby: Two diamonds.

Fanshawe: Three, no trumps.

Cuthbert: I say what do you think? We've struck an iceberg – a real big one – but there's no danger – no panic – an officer told me so.

Carruthers: Ice you say? No bid.

Maltravers: What does the fellow say the trouble is? Four, no trumps.

Fanshawe: Icebergs –

Digby: Well it can't be anything serious. No bid.

Cuthbert: If you care to see it, I'll take you up on the front bit and show you, the damn floor is littered with ice.

Maltravers: He means the deck. I'll go – after all I am dummy.

Cuthbert: There are tons of ice at the sharp end – come on.

Maltravers: Well that shouldn't harm us any. Come on and show me.

Fanshawe: Good Lord! No wonder he went off. Look at the hand he was bidding on.

(*Tut-tuts all round.*)

Pickering: I say, you fellows. If I were you I'd turn out. She's making water lickerty-spit – and the squash court is getting filled up.

(*Cast on stage 'freeze', Spirit enters stage right and moves across stage and exits.*)

Spirit: 'Tis all a Chequer-board of Nights and Days
Where Destiny with Men for pieces plays.
Hither and thither moves, and mates, and slays,
And one by one back in the Casket lays!'

(*Jenkins, a member of the crew, moves to the steerage group.*)

Jenkins: Right then, you steerage passengers – on the deck, double quick – lifebelts on – Captain's orders. Come on don't 'ang about!!

(*A variety of questions in foreign languages.*)

Jenkins: Oh blimey! Trust me to 'ave to deal wiv the bleedin' foreigners. Look – come 'ere – ship, shippee – us (*Mime*) – iceberg – cold – big (*Mime*) crash bang ship run into iceberg – ship down – in water, wet, nasty, cold – any bloody minute now – so let's have you all on deck – pronto!

(*A variety of foreign responses and panic from all on stage. Captain enters from stage right. The cast quieten down and group towards the rear of the stage.*)

Captain (*Sings*):
A gallant ship was lab'ring
Lab'ring in the sea;
The Captain stood amongst his crew
'Gather around' said he.
This ship is doomed and sinking,
Far on the lee is land,
Then launch the boats and pull away
But here at my post I'll stand
Goodbye my lads goodbye!
Goodbye my lads goodbye!

All (*Cast singing along with the Captain*):
I'll stick to the ship, lads, you save your lives
I've no one to love me, you've children and wives;

You take to the boats, lads, praying to Heav'n above,
But I'll go down in the angry deep, with the ship I love.

(*Applause from cast. Comedian enters stage right. M.C. enters stage left, they meet centre.*)

Comedian: I say, I say, I say, what do you get if you crossbreed elephants with mice?

M.C.: I don't know what do you get if you crossbreed elephants with mice?

Comedian: Bigger holes in your skirting board and your watertight compartments!

(*Comedian exits stage right, M.C. exits stage left. A group comes forward from the rear to represent ladies in the First Class Saloon: the Steward hovers stage left with coffee pot.*)

Lucinda: But, Mummy darling, why on earth can't *we* stay for port?

Gertrude: Good heavens, child, what a lot you have to learn, only the men stay for port.

Mabel: And cigars, of course.

Gertrude: Good Lord, don't put ideas like that into her head – she'll be wanting to smoke next.

Agatha: Not those foul cigarette things, surely?

Gertrude: I sincerely hope not, my dear.

Mabel: Steward, we'll take our coffee over here.

Steward: Very good ma'am. I'll be with you in a moment.

Dora: In a moment, he says – what is the line coming to?

Agatha: It's certainly not what it used to be and that's a fact.

(*The Steward comes over: the ripping sound is repeated.*)

Gertrude: Take care, man! Now look what you have done!

Lucinda: Oh Mummy – and that was one of your new dresses.

Steward: I'm extremely sorry, ma'am – I don't know how that happened.

Dora: Clumsy oaf!

(*Ad-libbed comments: a Purser comes forward from rear group.*)

Purser: Excuse me, ladies. We are in the North and have struck an iceberg. It does not amount to anything but will probably delay us a day getting into New York. However, as a matter of form the Captain has ordered all ladies on deck.

(*Ad-libbed comments and replies.*)

Teacher: All right! All right! We know there aren't lifeboats for everyone, but that's no excuse to behave like hooligans. Stop shuffling there! It's women and children first! – not yet, wait a moment, I'll tell you when – and remember its First Class first, then Second and then the rest – is that understood? Anyone who misbehaves will have to stay behind!

(*All cast on stage now form themselves into groups to represent six lifeboats and their passengers. The groups could be on six rostra, or be lit by six spotlights separately. There should be plenty of noise as these areas are set up, which in turn should stop on the whistle. With each whistle blown by the Teacher the action moves from boat to boat.*)

(*Whistle – Boat One*)

Stoker: Come on, move yourselves, move yourselves, look lively . . . . .

Woman: Are you in charge here?

Stoker: Yes mum, just move along will yer?

Woman: Certainly not – where's an officer? I demand we have an officer in charge.

(*Whistle – Boat Two*)

Officer: Women and children first! Women and children first!

Mrs Straus: Can my husband not join me?

Officer: He'll go in a later boat, ma'am.

Mrs Straus: If he cannot go with me then I don't go.

Mr Straus: But my dear, it would be more sense . . .

Mrs Straus: I'm sure nobody would object to an old gentleman like you getting in . . .

Mr Straus: I will not go before the other men.

Mrs Straus: . . . and if you stay I stay. I've always stayed with my husband; so why should I leave him now?

(*Whistle – Boat Three*)

Lady: My jewels! I've left my jewels.

Man: Keep still there! Damn you – you're rocking the whole boat.

Lady: But I can't leave my jewels – they're in my cabin.

Maid: I'll get them, ma'am.

Man: The boat won't wait.

Lady: Oh! and don't forget my furs, and my handcase, and my wrap, and my . . .

(*Whistle – Boat Four*)

Gentleman: Get back, it's First Class here only.

Foreigner: (*Replies in a foreign language.*)

Gentleman: Buzz off. You're Third Class – steerage – you'll have to wait.

Foreigner: (*Replies indicating his female companion*)

Gentleman: All right! She can come in, but you'll have to wait.

(*The couple are forcibly separated.*)

(*Whistle – Boat Five*)

Countess: Is there no officer here? No seaman to take control?

Woman 2: Not as yet.

Countess: Isn't it typical? Move over – give me the tiller.

Woman 2: Can you manage?

Countess: We'll see, won't we? Don't just sit there – take to the oars.

Woman 2: But . . .

Countess: No 'buts' – it's take to the oars or drown!

(*Whistle – Boat Six*)

Lady (*Screams*): It's a man!

Officer: Come on – out you come!

Man (*Panic*): Let me stay! Please let me stay! I can't swim. Let me stay!

Officer: Out – now! Don't make me use a gun on you.

(*Whistle – all boats. The scenes briefly indicated are improvised to a conclusion with others joining in.*)

(*A group begins singing 'Nearer my God to Thee'.*)

Nearer, my God, to thee,
Nearer to thee,
Even though it be a cross
That raiseth me
Still all my song shall be,
Nearer, my God, to thee,
Nearer to thee.

(*As the singing grows, the 'boats' join in.*)

Though, like the wanderer,
The sun gone down.
Darkness be over me,
My rest a stone;
Yet in my dreams I'd be
Nearer, my God, to thee
Nearer to thee.

(*As the second verse is sung the lights on the stage dim to out. The Narrator moves forward right and the Singer forward left.*)

Narrator (*In darkness*): At 2.20 a.m. the *Titanic* sank. It had taken less than three hours for the unsinkable liner to go down.

(*The lights come back up slowly.*)

Singer: At 4.00 a.m. the *Carpathia* arrived at the last known position of the *Titanic*. The survivors were taken aboard.

(*Members of cast as survivors who moved off stage in the darkness are helped back on.*)

Narrator: There were seven hundred and three survivors.

Singer: Fifteen hundred and three lives were lost.

(*Spirit enters at rear of stage, on a high level.*)

Spirit: 'The moving finger writes; and, having writ,
Moves on: nor all thy Piety nor Wit
Shall lure it back to cancel half a Line,
Nor all thy Tears wash out a Word of it.'

Singer (*Sings*):
A Big ship left port on its first maiden voyage,
The world gaz'd in wonder and pride . . . . .
Old England was proud of the ship and its crew
Whose Captain was trusted and tried . . . . .

The ship was a city of splendour and light,
Its rich and its poor side by side . . . . .
But when the shock came and the vessel went down,
Rich man and poor man like Englishmen died.

All (*Sing*):

On the Ship that will never return . . .
The Ship that will never return . . .
Brave words were spoken, and brave hearts were broken.
Ah! Here's where true love you discern . . .
Mothers they sobb'd in pray'r . . .
As they parted from lov'd ones there . . .
Husbands and sons, brave-hearted ones,
On the ship that will never return . . .

(*The Teacher moves to centre at front of stage.*)

Teacher: Homework – now take this down – and don't pull faces like that as soon as homework is mentioned – you're here to learn, remember.

(*All cast on stage sit down in groups as convenient.*)

'Why did the *Titanic* sink?'
'Why were there insufficient life-saving facilities?'
'Why did the *Californian* ignore the appeal for help?'

And I expect at least three sides . . . (*Cast moan*)
. . . and don't moan about it.

(*M.C. enters stage left, Comedian stage right. They meet centre.*)

M.C.: Ladies and Gentlemen . . . as I said earlier I'd like to perform for you a little recitation – a recitation entitled 'The Wreck of . . .'

Comedian: Here I say! You there! Yes you!

M.C.: Not now, not now – can't you see I'm busy – I'm just about to recite 'The Wreck of the Hesperus'.

Comedian: I thought you'd done that.

M.C.: No – we did the *Titanic* instead.

Comedian: Did it go down well?

All (*Standing, sing*):

O they built the ship *Titanic* to sail the ocean blue
And they thought they had a ship that the water would never go through.
But the Lord's almighty hand knew that ship would never land.
It was sad when that great ship went down.

It was sad (it was sad),
It was sad (mighty sad),
It was sad when that great ship went down.
Husbands and wives, little children lost their lives
It was sad when that great ship went down.

(*Repeat chorus at least once more*)

CURTAIN

Drama ideas

1 Work in a small group of three or four. One of you is a reporter covering the first voyage of the *Titanic* for a national newspaper. The others in the group are passengers from the First Class, the Second Class and Steerage. The reporter questions each passenger in turn about their impressions after their first day on board the ship.

2 Work with a partner. Imagine that you are two radio operators on the *Titanic*, Harold Bride and Jack Phillips. What happens when, after the disaster, Bride suggests sending the new call sign 'S.O.S.', instead of the usual 'C.D.Q'?

3 Work in a group of four or five. You are the people in one of the lifeboats after the disaster. Some of you are very anxious to return to the scene to search for survivors. Others are afraid that the lifeboat may also sink. Decide what your attitude is, and the reasons which lie behind it, before your scene begins.

4 Imagine that after the loss of the *Titanic*, a public inquiry is being held into the disaster. Working as a whole class, or perhaps in smaller groups, decide who will be on the board of inquiry, and who will be the various people giving evidence. You may choose to be some of the characters in the play, and your teacher might play the role of the Chairman of the Board of Inquiry. Who will be blamed for the disaster?

Follow-up work

1 Imagine that you are a survivor of the disaster. You were travelling on the liner with a companion who went down with the ship. It is your job to write and inform their next of kin of the death. What will you tell your friend's relatives about how your friend died? Are there any details you can include which may make the relatives feel better about their loss?

2 Imagine that you are a doctor who examined some of the survivors after they had been rescued. Write a medical report on one or two of the passengers, in which you describe their condition and the effects on them of the tragedy.

3 Try to find out what happened to the Lusitania, another great liner which sank. Its story is in many ways even more dramatic than that of the Titanic.

4 Collect newspaper stories and historical accounts of great disasters, which happened both recently and in the past, and make a class anthology. Which disasters were caused purely by accident and which ones might have been prevented?

5 The quickest way of sending messages used to be the telegram. In a telegram you paid for every word you used, and 'STOP' had to be used to show the end of sentences or phrases. Imagine that you can only send a twelve-word telegram and draft one that might have been sent from a member of the crew to his wife, explaining about the disaster, and saying that he is safe, although he has no idea when he will be home.

Try writing a telegram announcing the loss of the ship to the directors of the Cunard Line. Use as few words as possible.

6 The *Titanic* has been found recently, resting at the bottom of the North Atlantic. The possibility of raising the ship to the surface is being explored, although scientists and engineers fear that this may not be possible.

Write a diver's-eye view of how the ship might look, as if you were one of those who went down to investigate it.

For discussion

1 It was only after the loss of the *Titanic* that it was considered vital for ships to have a wireless operator on duty for twenty-four hours of the day. After the disaster the regulations were changed and it was compulsory to provide an adequate number of lifeboats for all ships. Regular checks were also instituted on icebergs in the Atlantic, with warnings being issued by special patrols.

It often seems the case that regulations are not altered or rules made until a disaster occurs. Think of recent examples of this, e.g. acid rain, over-large oil-tankers, the storage of nuclear waste, etc.

2 At a time when the movement for women's equality was gaining strength, how was it that women were sent first into the lifeboats? Do you think that this would still happen today? Do you think this kind of arrangement is the correct one?

3 The story of the disaster contains many examples of bravery – in many different ways. As the ship sank, the orchestra played right to the end.

Do you think that this was uncommonly brave or uncommonly foolish? Think of some examples of behaviour in a similar situation which you would regard as outstandingly brave.

Reference books

Walter Lord, *A Night to Remember* Penguin
Lawrence Beesley, *The Loss of the* Titanic
Wyn Craig Wade, *The* Titanic. *End of a Dream*
Richard Garrett, *Stories of Famous Ships* Barker

Sources for music

'Rule, Britannia': Arne
'Oh, 'twas in the Broad Atlantic' by Michael Watson
'The 'Titanic'' (No composer's name available)
'Biggest Boat, yet Afloat': to the tune of 'Any Old Iron' (Darewski)
'The Ship I Love' by Felix McGlennon
Ragtime music leading into:
'Nearer my God to Thee' (Hymn)
'The Ship that will never Return' by F. V. St Clair.

The Godmother

The real Bonnie Parker (of Bonnie and Clyde)

Introduction

'The Godmother' owes its origin to the enthusiasm that greeted the film *Bugsy Malone*. (The play originally had the title 'Mugsy Balloon'.) It is a completely fictitious 'historical documentary' – the events that it relates never actually happened.

The storyline is perhaps not too ludicrous for the 'Roaring Twenties' period in American history, however. Some historians might well comment that the 1920s were a period of reaction against the harsh realities of the First World War. There was, both in Europe and America, a brief era of what could be called 'silliness' – a 'gaudy, bawdy, totally desperate decade' – which produced 'The Jazz Age', the growth of Hollywood, Prohibition, the Gangsters, and dances such as The Charleston and The Black Bottom.

In America it was Prohibition that aroused most passion. This was the banning of the manufacture and sale (but not consumption) of alcoholic drink. It was an attempt to put an end to drunkenness, but the attempt failed. Drink was smuggled into the country, or made secretly and illicitly, by gangs who soon became rich and powerful. Springing out of this gangland operation came associated criminal activities – drug-peddling, prostitution, enforced 'protection', and widespread gambling. Gangs became very strong and powerful, police forces and authorities often became corrupt and the whole atmosphere in the big American cities seems to have had a frantic 'live-for-today' and 'who cares' attitude.

The period has been well documented on stage and particularly on film, not only in the stylish humour of Damon Runyon's stories as portrayed in the musical *Guys and Dolls* and the humour of the more recent film *Some Like It Hot*, but also in 1930s screen versions of American gangster life such as *Little Caesar*, *The Public Enemy* and *Scarface*. It is estimated that over three hundred films have been made about the gangster era in America. There does seem to be some intention at times to glamorise this vicious period of American social history and we ought not to forget that characters such as Al Capone, Frank Nitti and Legs Diamond were ruthless individuals, most of whom were closely associated with the Mafia.

However, the characters in this play are very pale versions of their namesakes and, although violence is hinted at, the overall intention is to parody the period. It is a 'spoof' documentary.

Staging the play

It is vital that any performance of this play establishes the 'style' of the 'Roaring Twenties'. The dialogue should help capture the petty criminal and somewhat 'seedy' nature of the characters. Try to use American accents and to overplay your characters as much as possible. Overplaying a part is frequently referred to as 'hamming it up', and this play needs all the 'ham' that you can give it. Talking directly to the audience is a most important aspect of Spats Valetta's part. He is our narrator as well as our chief character, and he is an all-time 'loser'; he should also gain the audience's sympathy fairly quickly.

Velma is the 'brains' behind the whole plot. It should be readily apparent that she and the other girls have the men in the play exactly where they want them. It is a triumph for women's liberation in many ways – for the men are so ineffectual.

With the exception of Velma all the girls could attempt using a rather high-pitched voice, a sort of 'little-girl' voice that seems to add to the atmosphere. The character of many of the girls is suggested in their lines, and the actresses concerned should try to determine how strong, or coy, they are going to play the individual roles.

There are two basic locations for the play, the first scene being Spats' Theatrical Agency and the second being Big Joe's Elbow Room. The Director will need to decide how best this can be achieved on stage. If your stage has a large apron to it then you could play the office in front of the main curtain with the nightclub already set behind the curtain. You should try as far as possible to avoid any undue pausing at the scene-change, for once a slick pace has been established it really needs to become more frantic and farcical as the play progresses.

The music should be live if possible. A piano and drum accompaniment works well, and the musicians appear in both scenes. It would be possible for them to be on stage throughout if the director so wished, and for them to be suitably costumed.

The costuming is not easy: it should be in period as far as possible. Twenties dresses are a necessity for all the girls, together with long strings of beads and the head-band with upright feathers! Try to do a little research into period costume, and aim for authenticity.

Gunshots and a telephone bell are the only sound effects required and for these a starting pistol and an electric bell rung from offstage should work adequately. Do remember, however, that starting pistols do seem to be prone to failing just when you need them, so that you may need the stand-by of a flat length of wood with which to slap the stage for the necessary shots.

The Godmother

The characters

Spats Valetta - an out-of-work theatrical agent
Velma his Secretary

Alice **Lucy** **Inga** **Frances** **Laura** **Tallulah**	Show girls

Nick (the Stoat) Berkowitz - a petty criminal

Gloria **Dolores** **Lily** **Carmen** **Rita** **Miranda**	Another group of Showgirls

John (the Greek) - another petty criminal
Scarface - yet another petty criminal
Boss Lugano - the Boss!

Theda **Alma** **Mary**	- Boss Lugano's 'Broads'

The first performance by the Dewsbury Arts Group (Youth section)

The piano plays a snatch of Scott Joplin – possibly 'The Entertainer' – and a spotlight picks up the figure of Spats Valetta, down on his luck. He is dressed as a tramp. He searches the floor for cigarette ends, as he bends down to pick one up, he notices the audience – he straightens up and talks to them.

Spats: Some of the more discernin' amongst youse may well have realised that I am an all-time loser. Yeah – you're right, it shows – and some! Some wise guy once remarked that if brains was gunpowder Spats Valetta wouldn't have enough to blow his hat off. Spats Valetta! That's me. . . . And who quoted that little pearl of wisdom? . . . One of my best friends, that's who. . . . At least I thought she was one of my best friends . . . when she worked for me, that is . . . when I worked . . . when I was Spats Valetta, the great Theatrical Agent . . .

(*Lights up on Theatrical Agency. Stage left, there is a desk and chair, phone on desk; and a row of six chairs. A screen at the rear of the desk. Spats goes behind the screen.*)

Velma (*On 'phone*): . . . Mr Valetta's agency. Can I help you? . . . No I'm sorry, Mr Valetta ain't here as yet, could I take a message . . . who shall I say called? Sorry I can't quite hear you . . . could you spell it please? . . . Fred . . . yeah got that . . . A-S-T-A-I-R-E . . . OK. Mister Astaire, I'll see Mr Valetta gets your name. (*Puts phone down, tears up the paper on which she wrote the name.*) Some chance you have – we're up to our ears in hoofers . . .

Spats (*Putting his head round the screen*): See what I mean about *thinking* she was one of my best friends . . . dumb broad!

Velma (*Doing her nails and singing*):
Home in Pasadena . . .
Home where grass is greener,
Where honey bees, hum melodies,
And orange trees scent the breeze . . .

(*Phone rings.*)

Velma: Hello! Mister Valetta's Theatrical Agency. . . . Naw . . . he ain't here. . . . How should I know? . . . I ain't his keeper, I'm just his secretary . . . Keep your wool on, baby . . . Who shall I say called? . . . Sam who? . . . Goldwyn . . . OK . . . and you, you great hunk!

(*Tears up his name as she rings off.*)

Spats (*Peering round again*): . . . and to think I could have been in movies.

(*Phone rings.*)

Velma: Hello! Mister Valetta's The—. . . . oh Myrna, I'm so glad you rang. . . . Naw, he's still sleeping it off somewhere. . . . Yeah, he should take more water with it. . . . Yeah, you're right. . . . I should say. . . .

(*Group of six Showgirls enters from right talking and laughing and sit on the row of chairs. They check their make-up in small make-up compacts.*)

Velma: . . . I know Myrna . . . and I. . . . Yeah Myrna. . . . Yeah. . . . Just a moment, Myrna . . . (*To Showgirls*) Will you lot just can it for a moment, can't you see I'm on the telephone? . . . (*The Showgirls quieten.*) . . . Sorry, Myrna . . . some broads just blew in. . . . I don't know, it'll be for Spats. . . . Yeah. . . . I tell 'em all the time . . . getting work in Chicago is like getting pork chops at a kosher butcher's. . . . Yeah, some hopes . . . I don't know why Spats goes on in this business. . . . yeah. . . . You're right, Myrna . . . what else could he do?. . . I know. . . . He's the worst agent in all Chicago . . . I tell everybody. . .

Spats (*Peering round again*): . . . No wonder business was bad.

(*Showgirls, who have been listening, get up to go.*)

Velma: . . . Hey, hold it . . . where d'you think you're going?

Alice: . . . Well . . . er, we just thought, after what you said that . . . perhaps we should try another agency.

Velma (*Menacing*): . . . Sit down, take the weight off your heads . . . Who d'you think you are? . . . Do you know who's on the end of this wire? . . . No, course you don't! Well, I'll tell you, you dumbclucks. It's Myrna Kowolski, that's who, secretary to Mr Oscar Lewenstein . . . that's who . . .

Lucy (*The coy one.*): Who's he?

Velma: Only another agent, that's all . . . and we don't want him to know what business is really like, do we? . . .

Spats (*Peering round again*): Maybe I misjudged her . . .

Velma: . . . So sit tight, sister, and button your lip . . . Sorry, Myrna . . . some creep just came in with an escape act and I had to give him the bum's rush. . . . What? . . . Oh, I dunno, someone called Harry Houdini or something . . . no . . . I'd never heard of him, either . . .

(*Enter Spats from behind screen, having changed from his tramp outfit to a rather slick outfit.*)

Spats: Morning, Velma!

Showgirls (*Ad lib*): Oh, Mr Valetta, about your ad in the *Tribune*.
Mister Valetta, we're from the Aldo Nage Dancing Academy.
Do you think we could audition for you?
Oh, Mr Valetta we want so much to go on stage.
Can you help us, Mr Valetta?
Is there a chance for us?
Some opening?
We'll go anywhere.

Lucy: *We'll do anything. . .* (*Looks from others.*). . . within reason.

All girls: *Please, Mr Valetta!*

(*Velma carries on an ad lib phone call throughout this.*)

Spats: Please girls, I'm overwhelmed. Give me time . . . the mail, and the calls . . . Just take a seat . . . then I'll see what we can do for you . . . all. . . . A moment . . . please.

(*Showgirls sit down again.*)

Velma: . . . OK, Myrna . . . 'bye!

Spats: Who was that?

Velma: My sister in Detroit.

Spats (*To audience*): Just when I thought I could trust her!

(*Spats takes the seat at the desk as Velma vacates it.*)

Velma: Here's the mail. A letter from the delicatessen, he wants his dough. A letter from the tailor – he wants his dough. A letter from the landlord – he wants his dough.

Spats: Thank heavens for that, Velma! I thought they wanted my dough. (*He laughs.*)

Velma (*To audience*): Now you know why he failed in vaudeville!

Spats: Any calls?

Velma: I ain't finished with the mail.

Spats: Oh!

Velma: And a letter from someone who calls himself Boss Lugano of the Purple Gang . . . saying you owe him 'for booze and gambling debts and if you don't pay up you will be wearing a cement overcoat with lead facings and bullet trimmings which will not be the most helpful when we throw you in the lake . . .'

Spats (*Poleaxed*): Boss Lugano! . . . . . .!

Velma: And a letter from the Dog Pound. . . . Mister Valetta, are you OK?

Spats: Boss Lugano!

Velma: Can I get you anything, Mr Valetta?

Spats: Velma!

Velma: Yeah!

Spats: It's Boss Lugano!

Velma: I know, I read the letter.

Spats: What'll I do, Velma?

Velma: Well, there's these broads waiting to audition. . . .

Spats: Boss Lugano . . .

Velma: I'll get 'em in . . . it'll take your mind off your problems. . . .

Spats: Boss. . . .

Velma: OK, girls, let's see what you do. . . . Give the pianist your music. All together, are you . . . what's your names?

(*The Showgirls take off their coats. They are all dressed similarly for their routine.*)

Alice (*Passing the music*): Alice.

Lucy: Lucy.

Inga: Inga.

Frances: Frances.

Laura: Laura.

Tallulah: Tallulah.

Velma: Tallulah! Some name! You'll have to change that baby, you'll never get on in show business with a name like that!

Spats: Velma . . . get me a drink.

Velma: Sure, Mr Valetta . . . two aspirins or one? . . . Play the music, Harry. . . . Take it away, girls.

(*Velma goes out stage right. Harry plays, the Showgirls sing, Spats sits dazed.*)

Showgirls (*Sing 'That's My Weakness Now'.*):
'Love, love, love, love. What did ya do to me?
The things I never missed, are things I can't resist!
Love, love, love, love. Isn't it plain to see?
I just had a change of heart – What can it be?

She's got eyes of blue, I never cared for eyes of blue,
But she's got eyes of blue, And that's my weakness now!
She's got dimpled cheeks, I never cared for dimpled cheeks,
But she's got dimpled cheeks, And that's my weakness now!
Oh my! Oh me! Oh I should be good, I would be good, but gee!
She likes to bill and coo, I never liked to bill and coo,
But she likes to bill and coo; And that's my weakness now!

(*The song is sung as a routine, with gestures and simple moves. The girls are enthusiastic rather than good. They are all breathless at the end.*)

Alice (*Breathlessly*): Well, what d'you think, Mr Valetta?

Velma (*Re-entering with glass of water and aspirins*): He'll let you know.

Alice: What d'you mean, 'He'll let us know'? I'm talking to him not you, little Miss Bigshot.

Velma (*Giving glass and aspirins to Spats*): I speak for Mr Valetta.

Alice: Not as far as I'm concerned, you don't, sister.

Velma: Don't 'sister' me . . . you dummy . . .

Alice: Now see here, you answerin' service . . .

Velma: Sap! Dumbo!

Alice: Button your lip!

Velma: OK, you asked for it.

(*Velma and Alice make as if to mix it.*)

Spats: Hold it! OK, everybody, hold it right there. I got problems enough without you two adding to it . . . Velma, get on the phone, get me Boss Lugano . . .

Velma: Sure thing, Mr Valetta.

Spats: And you . . . what's your name . . .?

Alice: Alice . . .

Spats: Alice . . . you get ready to audition . . .

Alice: What?

Spats: 'Audition' I said . . . what you got for ears? – pretzels?

Lucy (*Sexily*): But we just did, Mr Valetta.

Spats: Call me 'Spats'.

Alice: We just did, 'Spats'.

Spats: *You* call me Mr Valetta. (*To Lucy*) You tell me.

Lucy: We just did our audition piece, Spatsy baby . . .

Spats: You did? Where was I?

Velma: In a state of shock . . . like most times. . . . Mister Lugano for you . . . Spatsy baby!

Spats: Cut that out, Velma. . . . The rest of you stick around . . . (*Slaps Lucy's bottom. Takes 'phone*) Hullo! Is that you, Boss? . . . Oh, I meant Mr Lugano . . . it's Spats here . . . Spats . . . S-P-A-T-S. . . . Yeah, that's it, Fink Valetta (*The Showgirls laugh.*) . . . About this little problem we have. . . . Yeah, sorry, I meant that . . . *I* have . . . could you just see your way. . . . I mean if you give me a little more . . . I mean . . . but . . . how . . . wh . . . er. . . . (*Puts 'phone down.*) . . . I . . . er . . . think we were cut off. Now where was I . . .?

Velma: Auditioning . . .

Spats: Oh yeah! Well . . . what d'you do?

Alice: Sing and dance.

Spats: D'you do cakes?

Lucy: Cakes?

Velma: Jumpin' out of cakes at birthdays.

Lucy: I suppose we could.

Velma: What about speakeasies?

Inga: Ve do anyting!

Velma: Not a Polak are you?

Inga: I a vrom Holland . . . I am Dutch . . .

Velma: Could've been worse, you could've been from the Bronx.

Frances: And what's wrong with the Bronx?

Spats: OK, cool it, all of you . . . Velma, what we got in the way of work?

Velma: Not much. One ventriloquist needed for a Church Tea Party over at 58th . . . and lemme see – oh yeah, we got a dancing/singing group needed for the burlesque show over at Big Joe's Elbow Room. . . .

Alice: We'll take it. . . .

Velma: You ain't been offered it . . .

Laura: We'll do it anyway. . . .

Lucy: Won't we Spatsy baby? . . .

Spats (*To audience*): That's what we call a delicate situation . . . fortunately it was eased by the arrival of Boss Lugano's chief messenger boy . . . Nick (the Stoat) Berkovitz. . . .

(*Back into scene.*)

Showgirls (*ad lib*): Come on, Spats, we can do it . . .
Give us a break.
Don't hold out on us.
C'mon Spats.

Velma (*Ad lib*): You ain't the only pebbles on the beach . . . Hold back there . . . who d'you think you are . . .

(*Enter Nick (the Stoat) stage right; he is very small.*)

Nick: Hi, Spats!

Showgirls (*Ad lib with awe*): It's Nick Berkovitz! It's the Stoat! It's Nick the Stoat!

(*They go back to their places and put coats on.*)

Spats: Nick . . . good to see yah! Beat it, baby . . . this is man's talk . . .
(*Velma ignores him.*
Nick walks over to Spats's desk. The Showgirls cower away from him.)

Nick (*To Velma*): . . . go and powder yer nose.

Velma: But I gotta . . .

Nick: Do it . . . or you won't have no nose to powder. . . .

Velma (*As she goes*): . . . OK, I'm going . . . I'm going . . .

Nick: . . . and take these other dames wid ya . . . powder their noses as well. . . .

(*The Showgirls and Velma all exit stage right.*)

Nick: Now then, Spats!

Spats: Now then, Nick . . .

Nick: The Boss sends his regards.

Spats: Thanks, Nick . . .

Nick: I ain't finished . . . and says that if you don't pay the dough you owe . . . then as sure as Sing-Sing you are gonna be one dead theatrical agent . . . the Boss says.

Spats: I get the message.

Nick: And what's more, he says don't forget to deliver the chicks to Big Joe's Elbow Room on time for the show tonight – otherwise he would be equally annoyed. . . .

Spats: I got that message too.

Nick: So where are they?

Spats: They were here just a minute ago when you came in. . . .

Nick: I never saw any chicks. . . .

Spats: But . . .

Nick: I don't see anybody when I'm working, except those I gotta see . . .

Spats: Yeah but . . .

Nick: No 'buts' . . . Just get 'em for tonight – and the dough. (*He moves right.*) Don't forget, Spats . . . or there'll be a vacancy in the Theatrical Press for an agent – and you won't be around to apply for it.

(*Nick exits stage right. Spats mops his brow at stage left.*)

Spats (*To audience*): You never argue with Nick the Stoat. (*To offstage*): OK, girls, let's have you in.

(*A different group of six girls enters from the right.*)

Spats (*Walking back to desk*): Give your music to Harry . . . and start when you're ready.

(*He sits at his desk and hides behind the Boss Lugano letter. The new girls take off coats and perform their routine: 'Ain't she Sweet'.*)

Showgirls (2): Ain't she sweet? See her coming down the street!
Now I ask you very confidentially – ain't she sweet?
Ain't she nice? Look her over once or twice.
Now I ask you very confidentially – ain't she nice?
Just cast an eye in her direction.
Oh me! Oh my! Ain't that perfection?
I repeat don't you think that's kind of neat?
And I ask you very confidentially – ain't she sweet?

Spats (*Still wrapped up in the letter*): Yeah! OK, you'll do . . .

(*Girls respond with shouts, etc.*)

Take a seat . . . I'll get my secretary to book you officially . . . you start tonight at Big Joe's Elbow Room. (*Shouts*) Velma!

(*Velma enters stage right, followed by the original six Girls.*)

Velma: What're you screamin' about . . .

Spats: Book this group for the Elbow job.

(*Velma looks at the new six, then the original six, who also look at the new six.*)

Spats (*To audience*): Can you imagine the argument there was then . . .?

BLACKOUT

(*During which we hear various fight sounds and ad libs, e.g. 'Hands off our job', 'Keep your elbows to yourself', 'Spats, you fink', 'Take that . . .', 'It's our job . . .', 'You . . . dumbo . . .', 'Cheapskate . . .', 'It ain't fair . . .*

you slob'. . . 'Take this, you . . . job stealers', . . . 'Blacklegs'. When the lights go up again, Spats is centre, very much kicked about – the two girl-groups pose right and left, somewhat disarrayed, but swinging handbags, Velma very cool at the desk.)

Spats: Velma! I can't take any more.

Velma: OK, girls, hold it there . . . I think you've made your point clear to Mr Valetta.

Spats: Thanks, Velma!

Alice: So when do we get round to finishing him off, Velma?

Inga: Just sa ze vord und I vill extingvish him myzelf.

Gloria: Lemme have first swing, sister.

Laura: We was here first.

Dolores: But he gave *us* the job.

Tallulah: And now we're gonna give him the works.

All: Yeah! Lemme at him (*etc.*).

Velma: Hold it, girls! I think we can do better than that.

All: What d'you mean, Velma? (*etc.*)

(*Velma takes Spats back to his desk and sits him down.*)

Velma: Well, now, I reckon how you've just proved to me something that I believed all the time . . .

Dolores: Quit all this fancy talk – what d'you mean?

Alice: Yeah, stop shootin' the crap and start making sense – like she (*Indicates Lucy*) can understand.

Velma: Lucy – sit on Spats's knee – keep his mind on other things.

Lucy: Sure thing, Vel. (*She does and helps Spats regain his appearance.*)

Velma: Now listen, the rest of you . . . who rules Chicago? . . . Who's the Boss?

Lily: Lugano – Boss Lugano, Velma.

Velma: Why?

Rita: Are you kiddin? 'Cos he runs all the rackets . . . numbers . . .

Lily: Speakeasies.

Carmen: Girls.

Miranda: Booze.

Frances: Drugs.

Velma: Right! Right! And how does he do that? How does he keep himself at the top?

Alice: He's got a gang of heavies working for him.

Inga: Dey are doink all his dirty verk.

Gloria: Yeah . . . Lugano's hoodlums.

Velma: Well now – how would you like to be Spats Valetta's hoodlums?

Laura: What d'y'a mean?

Velma: Look at the way you set into Spats just now – another few minutes and he would have been doing a very good imitation of a strawberry flan . . . you could take anybody. . . .

(*Pause*.)

Alice: She's right.

Gloria: You betcha she's right.

Carmen: *We* could be hoodlums too.

Rita: It's the best part I've ever been offered by an agent.

Tallulah: So what do we do?

Lily (*Imitates a machine-gun*): . . . cut 'em down to size.

All: Yeah! (*Plus laughs and agreements.*)

Velma: But you got to look the part.

Alice: You mean dress as men . . .?

Velma: Rumour has it that hoodlums ain't women and we wouldn't want to get any innocent girls the blame surely?

(*More laughter all round.*)

Laura: I always wanted to be a man . . . on stage.

Frances: This is your best chance, darling. . . .

Rita: I've got a suit somewhere.

Tallulah: Me too.

Gloria: Let's face it, we've all got the clothes. . . .

Alice: So what are we waitin' for? Let's go get 'em. . . .

Velma: Hold it . . . hold it . . . (*They pause.*) . . . you can't *all* be men. Some have to do the singing and dancing.

Miranda: I knew there'd be a snag. . . .

Velma: Boss Lugano . . . *expects* some girls . . . he *expects* Spats Valetta . . . but we'll give him what he *don't* expect. What did you say your name was?

Alice: Alice.

Velma: So you're 'Big Al' . . . and you?

Inga: Inga from Holland.

Velma: So you're 'Dutch' . . . and you?

Frances: Frances.

Velma: That's easy – you're 'Frank' . . . and you?

Laura: Laura, but I'm called 'Lucky'.

Velma: That'll do fine . . . and you?

Tallulah: Tallulah!

Velma: Now you're 'Longy' and you over there?

Lily: Yeah? I'm Lily.

Velma: No – from here on you're 'Legs', OK?

Lily: OK by me.

Velma: So who're our hoodlums?

(*The girls step forward in turn.*)

Tallulah: Longy Zwillman.

Lily: Legs Diamond.

Laura: Lucky Luciano.

Frances: Frank Nitti.

Inga: Dutch Shultz.

Alice: Big Al Capone.

Spats (*To audience*): With names like that, how could we fail?

Velma: OK, girls away you go – get changed and meet at the Elbow Room at 11.30 – outside! *I'll* see that Spats is there.

Carmen: What about us, Velma?

Miranda: Do we see you there too?

Alice: Course you do, sugar – you'll be on stage – and you better be good.

Laura: Yeah! *We men* won't stand no nonsense.

Dolores: Buzz off, you ain't no gangster yet.

Miranda: Go draw yourself a moustache, wise guy.

Lily: Go draw yourself a pension!

Tallulah: And sing good, you songbirds!

Inga: Or ve vill gif you ze boird! A joke – no?

Velma: No! C'mon, Lucy, you too.

Lucy: By-ee, Spatsy baby!

(*All the girls and Velma go off stage right: phone rings.*)

Spats: Spats Valetta speakin' . . . What? Oh yeah, *Mr* Lugano . . . of course they'll be there . . . and me? . . . of course *I'll* be there . . . and the dough? . . .

(*A look at the audience, a shrug and Spats exits stage left. Nick, John the Greek, and Scarface enter stage right.*)

Nick: OK, youse guys, now you know what to do.

Scarface: What's dat, den Nick?

Nick: It's the protection, ain't it, Scarface? Protection!

John: Who're we protectin', Nick?

Nick: The Boss – who else? The Boss. Stay close to him.

Scarface: Where is he, Nick?

Nick: Where is he?

John: Yeah – where is he?

Nick: He'll be there at the Elbow Room – you just keep your eyes open, that's all.

John: Sure, Nick.

Nick: *I'll* go find the Boss and tell him that Spats is on the way. I'll meet you at the Elbow Room.

Scarface: I can hardly wait.

Nick: Listen, wise guy . . . you just do your job, get it?

Scarface: Sure ting Nick.

Nick: See that he does, Acropolis. (*He goes off, stage right.*)

John: OK, Nick.

Scarface: Acropolis? What kind of a name's that?

John: It's Greek. . . . *I'm* Greek . . . so what? You wanna make somethin' of it?

Scarface: Acropolis . . . fancy me not knowin' . . . some name.

John: See here, wise guy . . . you just cut that out or you'll have another reason to be called Scarface.

Scarface: Calm down . . . will you? . . . I didn't know, that's all . . .

John: . . . and anyway what's *your* name . . .?

Scarface: . . . Einstein . . . Izzy Einstein.

John (*To audience*): And I thought I had problems.

(*They exit stage right. The curtain opens on Big Joe's Elbow Room, the chairs are set by Theda, Alma and Mary at tables front left and right. A pianist plays a Scott Joplin rag. John and Scarface enter centre rear.*)

Scarface: Hiya, girls!

Theda: Get lost, you creep.

John: Someone who knows you well?

Scarface: I'm warning you . . . Apocalypse.

John: Acropolis! Acropolis!

Nick (*Entering centre rear*): OK, move it, move it . . . the Boss is on his way.

Girls (*Swooning*): Boss Lugano!

(*The Boss enters and takes his place at a table stage left, the Girls sit around him.*)

Theda: You sure know how to handle that Spats Valetta, Mr Lugano.

Boss: You can say that again!

Alma: And you know how to keep a girl happy.

Boss: You can say that again!

Mary: Ain't we lucky to have you around.

Boss: You can say that again!

Theda: That Spats owes you, Mr Lugano.

Boss: You can say that again!

Alma: All that dough, Mr Lugano.

Boss: You can say that again!

Mary: You got such a lovely way with words, Mr Lugano.

(*Pause*.)

Boss: You can say that again!

(*Nick walks across to the table*.)

Nick: Well, Boss, he's on his way . . .

Boss: You don't say!

Nick: I do say – sure thing – Velma's bringing him along.

Boss: You don't say!

Nick: He sure is scared, Boss.

Boss: You don't say!

Nick: You got him right where you want him.

Boss: You don't say!

Mary: You're so cute, Mr Lugano.

(*Pause*)

Boss: You can say that again!

Nick: I'll go keep an eye open for him. (*He exits stage left.*)

Theda: Ain't it time the girls were here, Mr Lugano?

Boss: You can say that again!

Alma: Ain't you ready for a show already?

Boss: You can say that again!

Theda: Spats Valetta promised them.

Alma: He said they'd be here.

Mary: It's time they were on, Mr Lugano.

(*Pause.*)

Boss: You can say that again.

(*Nick re-enters, centre rear.*)

Nick: Boss – Boss – Spats and Velma are here.

Boss: You don't say.

Nick: and . . .

Theda: and what?

Alma: What's the matter, Nick?

Mary: What is it, Stoaty?

Nick: Well . . . he . . .

Theda: Yeah?

Nick: He . . .

Theda:
Mary: } Yeah?

Nick: He . . .

Theda:
Mary:
Alma: } Yeah?

Nick: He . . .

Theda:
Mary:
Alma:
Scarface:
John: } Yeah?

Nick: If you'll keep quiet a minute I'll tell ya! . . . he's brought a whole gang of hoodlums with him . . .

Boss (*Pause*): You don't say!

(*Enter Spats and Velma from centre rear, crossing to stage right.*)

Spats: Evenin', Mr Lugano, Nick, . . . boys . . . girls!

Velma: Evenin' you all.

Spats: You don't know my . . . associates, do you? Lemme introduce you . . . Velma, do the honours. . . .

(*As Velma announces the girls, they enter and take up position stage right round table at which Spats sits; Laura carries a violin case.*)

Velma: Big Al . . . . . . Capone
Legs . . . . . . Diamond
Lucky . . . . . . Luciano.
Frank . . . . . . Nitti – next time leave your handbag at home, Frank . . .
Dutch . . . . . . Schultz.
Longy . . . . . . Zwillman.

(*Nick looks closely at 'Longy' as she crosses stage.*)

Nick (*Whistles*): You can say that again!

Boss: Stop pinchin' my lines, Nick. . . . Where are my boys?

Nick: Well, there's Acropolis and Einstein here . . .

Boss: Who?

John:
Scarface: } Us.

Boss: Oh yeah.

Nick: And I've sent the word out. . . . The rest are on the way . . .

Boss: Good thinkin', Nick. . . . We may need 'em later on.

Spats (*To audience*): I could see the Boss was planning somethin'.

Velma: He couldn't see farther than the end of the week . . . I *knew* Lugano was up to somethin'.

Boss (*Moving to centre stage*): Well, Spats . . . this is an honour . . .

Spats (*Joining the Boss at centre*): You can say that again!

Boss: Don't you start . . .

Spats: I don't get you.

Boss: Cut the garbage, Valetta, have you got the dough . . . or do I have to get the boys to fill you in . . .?

(*John and Scarface step forward.*)

Velma (*Announcing*): Mister Lugano, Ladies, Gentlemen and you too, Spats . . . your appreciation please for the Elbow Room Girls.

(*Applause. Spats and Boss return to their tables. Nick exits stage left. The Girls enter and perform their number and routine: 'Nobody's Sweetheart Now'.*)

Girls: You're nobody's sweetheart now
They don't baby you somehow.
Fancy hose, silken gown –
You'd be out of place in your own home town.
When you walk down the avenue
I just can't believe that it's you –

Painted lips, painted eyes –
Wearing a bird of Paradise.
It all seems wrong somehow
That you're nobody's sweetheart now!

(*At the end of the number Spats applauds wildly. The Girls take up positions at stage right and left.*)

Spats (*Stands*): More! More . . . wonderful . . . more . . . more . . . Bring 'em on again . . . more!

Alice: Sit down, Spats. You're showin' us up.

Boss: Yeah – he's right – can it, Spats.

(*Nick re-enters from stage left.*)

Are the rest of the boys here yet, Nick?

Nick: Sure thing, boss.

Boss: Would you like to step into my office, Spats?

Spats (*To audience*): Who could decline an invitation like that? Look after the shop, Velma.

Velma: Sure, Spats.

(*Spats crosses to Boss's table.*)

Spats: You wanted me, Mr Lugano?

Boss: Sit down!

(*John and Scarface sit him down.*)

Spats: Thanks, fellas!

Boss: It's the dough I want, Valetta . . . you owe me!

Alma: You tell him, Mr Lugano.

Boss: I ain't speakin' to you, sugar – so wrap up.

Alma: But . . .

Nick: You heard the Boss, . . . quit it!

Boss: Now, Spats . . . do I get my dough or do I call the rest of the boys in?

Spats: The rest? . . . How many?

Nick: Two here . . . four outside and then there's me!

Spats: Lemme have a word with Velma.

Boss: Do it!

Spats (*Crossing to Velma*): What'll I do now Velma? I ain't got the dough. Lugano's boys will finish me off. . . .

Velma: Keep him talking . . . we'll deal with his boys . . . won't we, girls?

Laura: No trouble, Vel. . . . Leave it to us!

(*General agreement from the rest. Spats returns to Boss.*)

Spats: What do I owe?

Boss: What does he owe, Einstein?

Scarface: 'Er . . . lemme see now, it'll be five and carry one . . . no it'll be four, no six thousand . . . no that's not right . . . lemme add it up again.

Boss: Nick . . . get the books . . .

Nick: Come wid me . . . Einstein!

(*They exit stage left, followed ominously by Laura with a violin case.*)

Spats: Nice place you have here.

Theda: Mister Lugano only has the best.

Boss: Wrap up, sugar.

Theda: I only said that you . . .

Boss: I heard what you said. . . . Did you hear what *I* said?

Theda: Sure, Mr Lugano . . . sorry, Mr Lugano.

(*Gunshot offstage – Nick re-enters from stage left.*)

Nick: Boss! Boss! Somethin' terrible's happened.

Boss: You don't say.

Nick: Scarface has just been shot.

(*Laura enters and walks back to her place – smiling. She hands her violin case to Lily.*)

Boss: Don't worry, we still got five, Nick . . .

Nick: And me!

Boss: Yeah!

Spats: Trouble, Mr Lugano?

Boss: Listen, wise guy . . . trouble don't worry me . . . it's my middle name. . . . I ain't got trouble, Valetta . . . it's you that's got all the trouble, if you don't produce the dough . . . you get me?

(*Lily exits stage left, giving John the 'eye'; he does a double take then follows.*)

Alma: You tell him, Mr Lugano . . .

Boss: I just did!

Mary: We heard, we heard!

Boss: So cough up, Spats!

Spats: Sure thing, Mr Lugano . . . of course, Mr Lugano . . . I'm going to, Mr Lu . . .

(*Another offstage shot and cry. Nick exits quickly stage left.*)

Boss: Or my five boys will see to you. . . . Get it?

Nick (*Re-entering*): Four, Boss.

Boss: What d'ya mean, 'four'?

Nick: The Greek's just bought it.

(*Lily re-enters smiling, and goes back to her place, handing the violin case to Frances.*)

Boss: . . . OK, so my four boys will take care of things . . .

(*Frances and Alice go out stage left.*)

Nick: . . . And me, Boss.

Alma: They can handle it, Mr Lugano.

Boss: Quiet! Dummy! I'll decide on the decisions round here . . . I'm still running this joint . . . nobody's gonna take Boss Lugano for a ride . . . d'ya hear me? . . . Well, d'ya hear me?

(*Two shots offstage and Frances and Alice return to their places. Nick exits stage left.*)

Boss: Tell me the worst, Nick.

Nick (*Re-entering*): We're down to two, boss.

Theda: . . . and you!

Boss: It's still enough. . . . Now, Spats . . . this is your last chance. . . . Hand over the green stuff.

(*Tallulah and Inga exit stage left with the violin case. Everyone pauses and waits, listening. . . . No noise, so the Boss continues.*)

Boss: C'mon, I ain't got all that much time to waste, you've kept me waiting for this dough for too long. . . . I've got better things to do with my time. . . .

(*Two shots ring out and appropriate shouts. Tallulah and Inga re-enter and shake hands with their gang stage right.*)

Boss: What do we do now, Nick?

Nick: Say, Spats – how'd'you like to book a new double act?

(*Nick and Boss are bundled out by the 'gangsters' and girls stage left, who then return.*)

Mary: What do *we* do now?

Alma: If you can't beat 'em, honey . . .

Theda: . . . join 'em.

(*Routine: 'So you wanna be a Gangster' – the song is punctuated by offstage cries from Nick and Boss . . . Spats sidles off stage right.*)

All (*Except Theda, Alma and Mary, sing*):
So you wanna be a gangster,
Wanna have a gun –
Play the horses and the numbers
Dare you have some fun?

Alice: Can you lie, can you cheat, can you beat up folk if you have to?
Can you steal, can you drink, do you think you can swear if you need to?

(*Theda, Alma and Mary shake their heads.*)

Well you might as well quit –
'Cos you haven't got it!

All (*Except Theda, Alma and Mary*):
So you wanna be a hoodlum
Where the livin's fat
Come along and call your best friend

Tallulah: Why you dirty rat!

Alice: Can you shoot, can you kick, can you stick up banks if you have to?
Can you laugh, can you smile, all the while that the cops try to break you?
Well you might as well quit –
'Cos you haven't got it!

Laura: Put 'em in the gang, Vel.
Make 'em one of us
They can be a man too –
Let 'em make a fuss

Theda
Alma
Mary
We'll show 'em the way
And make the guys pay.

Frances: Let 'em have a try Vel,
Show 'em what we're at –
Give 'em all a dark suit
And a Cagney hat –

All: They'll look like the rest
And soon pass the test
– For sure, Vel!

Alice: So you wanna be a mobster
Have a life of crime –
Make the most of crooked livin'
While you're in your prime.

Theda
Alma
Mary
We can fight, we can scratch, we can catch on to things very quickly –
We like mobs, we like crime all the time, even when things are sickly.
And we don't mean to quit
'Cos we've plenty of it!

Alice: Put 'em in with us, Vel,
Teach 'em all you can –
They can take 'em on Vel –
We'll be man to man.

Theda
Alma
Mary
Well, show us the way
We'll do what you say!

All (*Except Theda, Alma and Mary*):
They won't let us down Vel,
When they're in our mob –

Theda
Alma
Mary
You can count on us girls!

All (*Except Theda, Alma and Mary*): Now you've got a job!

All: We'll show all those rats
– Especially
–that fink
– SPATS!

(BLACKOUT – when lights come up, the cast are in a 'freeze'.)

Spats (*Re-enters at right, a tramp again; to the audience*): . . . And that's how it happened. . . . Velma took over the Agency . . . and the town. . . . Of course she had to take a new name too. . . . I can't remember what it was . . . apart from the fact that it reminded me of housework.

Velma (*On phone stage right*): Yeah . . . who d'you want? . . . J. Edgar Hoover? (*She puts on a trilby.*) . . . speakin'.

Spats: . . . and as for Nick and the Boss . . .

(*Nick and the Boss dressed as chorus girls appear centre rear and begin to sing – 'That's my weakness now'. The audience of the 'hoodlums' and real girls boo and give them the bird. Two of the girls give Nick and the Boss a well-aimed 'custard pie'. Cast go into a 'freeze' again.*)

Spats: I hate to think what they'll do to me if they ever catch me – reckon I'll change my name too . . .

(*He starts scratching.*)

Damn bugs! . . . Bugs! Hey, p'raps I could call myself . . . *Oliver Hardy. . . . That's another fine mess you've gotten me into, Velma!

(*Curtain chorus of 'That's my weakness now'.*)

*This line was originally 'Bugsy . . . Bugsy Malone . . . how far would I get with a name like that?' This final line can be changed to suit 'Spats' and the cast – by the time you get to this line you should have the 'style' of the play right enough to make your own decisions.

Drama ideas

1 Presumably Velma was interviewed by Spats for the job as his secretary. Working in twos, improvise this scene, in which she persuades Spats that there can be no doubt about the job being hers.

2 Imagine that you are a newspaper reporter. Work with your partner, who will take on the role of your editor. Dictate the story of the events at Big Joe's Elbow Room over the phone to your editor.

3 Work with a partner. Imagine that one of you works in the office next door to Spats and Velma. You have become suspicious about the things you overhear. Your partner is a close friend or relation, who thinks that sometimes you are inclined to exaggerate. Will you be believed when you describe what's been going on next door?

4 Work in a small group. One of you is a detective investigating the shootings at the nightclub. The rest of the group are the girls. How will they explain away what's been happening?

Follow-up work

1 Write a series of no more than six sensational headlines for an American newspaper that relate the main events of the play.

2 Draft the advertisement that Spats and Velma put in the theatrical press for a group of girls to appear at Big Joe's Elbow Room.

3 Most of the gangsters of this period seem to have had nicknames, many of them humorous or describing some personal characteristic. The American author Damon Runyon created many such names for the petty criminals he wrote about in his stories. Devise a gangland name for each of the people in your group.

4 It might be possible to obtain some recorded music of the period. Try to find some 'Charleston' music and discover some of the steps of the dance. You might even try a short routine.

For discussion

1 Dances like the 'Charleston', the 'Black Bottom' and even the 'Tango' were thought of as being decadent, even obscene, by the older generation of that time. What do the older generation today think about

dancing and music? How do you think young people today will react in the future when they become the older generation?

2 Al Capone said, 'Everyone calls me a racketeer. I call myself a businessman. When I sell liquor it's bootlegging. When my patrons serve it on Lake Shore Drive on a silver tray, it's hospitality'. How much sympathy do you have for his comments? How good an idea do you think Prohibition was?

3 The introduction of Prohibition was a genuine attempt to combat drunkenness and the long-term effects of alcohol. If we believe that smoking can be harmful to our health should not smoking be prohibited in the same way? How similar to the results of the prohibition of alcohol might the prohibition of cigarettes be?

4 Consider the current styles in music, fashion, and life styles. What aspects in the lives of young people today do you think will be looked back on as being 'silly' in ten or twenty years?

Reference books

The Twenties (a songbook), Chappell and Co. Ltd.
Damon Runyon on Broadway

Sources of music:

'Pasadena' by Clarke, Leslie & Warren (Lawrence Wright).
'That's my Weakness Now' by Green & Sept (Lawrence Wright).
'Ain't she Sweet' by Yellen & Ager (Lawrence Wright).
'Nobody's Sweetheart' by Kahn, Erdman, Meyers & Schoebel (Lawrence Wright).
'So you Wanna be a Gangster': parody of 'So you Wanna be a Boxer', from *Bugsy Malone* (Chappell Music).

The four plays in this volume were originally presented by the Dewsbury Arts Group (Youth Section), with the following casts:

A Memory of Lizzie

Susan Barnes, Debbie Brown, Julie Burroughs, Clare Cathcart, Sephora Disken, Sharon Ellis, Helen Green, Dawn Holt, Rachel Mellor, Stephanie Nicolaides, Anne Ramsden, Sarah Sykes, Georgina Todd, Stacy Tyson, Helen Warters, Debbie Webber, Anne Winder.

I was a Good Little Girl 'til . . .

Lynne Burnett, Clive Burroughs, Julie Burroughs, Tracy Burroughs, Clare Cathcart, Joanna Craig, Sephora Disken, Adrian Farrow, Andrew Firth, Shona Firth, Sophie Flynn, Beverley Hanson, Simon Harvey, Fiona Hetherington, Dawn Holt, Alison Kemp, Sarah Kemp, Catherine Knox, Tom Lynch, Jill Mitchell, Maria Mulrennan, Jacky Naylor, Heather Petyt, Jacqui Petyt, Simon Philpott, Louise Ragan, Louise Rawson, Linda Shaw, Gill Smith, Beverley Turner, David von Emloh, Jacqui Wicks, Anne Winder.

Titanic

Susan Barnes, Stephan Brooke, Debbie Brown, Clive Burroughs, Julie Burroughs, Tracy Burroughs, Clare Cathcart, Joanna Craig, Nicola Dawson, Jill Denvers, Susan Denvers, Katharine Disken, Mandy Edwards, Sharon Ellis, Adrian Farrow, Nigel Hawker, Stewart Hill, Karen Holt, Claire Ineson, Rebecca Jackson, Andrew Jennings, Wayne Lintott, Jane Lynch, Fiona McCormack, Rachel Mellor, Maria Mulrennan, Stephanie Nicolaides, Heather Petyt, Sarah Pinder, Louise Ragan, Anne Ramsden, Georgina Todd, Judith Walsh, Debbie Webber, Anne Winder, Richard Wood, David Wright.

The Godmother

Helen Connor, Susan Dillon, Sophie Drake, Morwenn Evans, Maxine Hartley, John Horne, Sarah Jackson, Chris Knowles, Michelle Knowles, Jessica Lake, Mark Lynch, Suzanne Middleton, Donna Ransome, Helen Rawson, Catherine Sheard, Sarah Taylor, Kay Thomlinson, Pamela Whiteley, Andrew Wood, Philippa Wood, Richard Wood.